4
Human Resources

Keith Brumfitt, Stephen Barnes, Liz Norris & Jane Jones

Vocational Business

4

Human Resources

Keith Brumfitt, Stephen Barnes, Liz Norris & Jane Jones

Series Editor: Keith Brumfitt

© Keith Brumfitt, Stephen Barnes, Liz Norris and Jane Jones 2001

Original illustrations © Nelson Thornes Ltd 2001

Published in 2001 by:
Nelson Thornes Ltd
Delta Place
27 Bath Road
CHELTENHAM
GL53 7TH
United Kingdom

01 02 03 04 05 / 10 9 8 7 6 5 4 3 2 1

A catalogue record for this book is available from the British Library

ISBN 0 7487 6362 7

Illustrations by Oxford Designers and Illustrators
Page make-up and illustrations by GreenGate Publishing Services, Tonbridge, Kent

Printed and bound in Italy by Stige

Contents

Introduction to Vocational Business series

This textbook is one of a series of six covering the core areas of business studies. Each book focuses on vocational aspects of business rather than theoretical models, allowing the reader to understand how businesses operate. To complement this vocational focus, each book contains a range of case studies illustrating how businesses respond to internal and external changes.

The textbooks are designed to support students taking a range of business courses. While each is free standing, containing the essential knowledge required by the various syllabuses and course requirements, together they provide a comprehensive coverage of the issues facing both large and small businesses in today's competitive environment.

Titles in the series

Acknowledgements

The authors and publishers would like to thank the following people and organisations for permission to reproduce photographs and other material:
PFD on behalf of Ros Asquith; Andrew Carruth/Famous; First Direct; the Ford Motor Company Ltd; Gemini Recruitment Group, Cheltenham; Guardian Newspapers Ltd; Joslin Rowe, Recruitment Consultants; Martin Sookias; Corel; Photodisc.

Every effort has been made to contact copyright holders and we apologise if any have been overlooked.

Human Resources

Introduction

This book gives you the skills to apply for a job and prepare for difficult interviews. It will guide you through the interview and help you to see things from the employer's perspective. It you want to get the job, this book will be your guide. It will also help you understand how employers decide when and where to recruit.

Human resources management is relevant to every type of job

1

| What is human resource management?

Your friends and family are all likely to have had some direct experience of major changes in their jobs. Even those who have been employed by the same company for a long time will have found that the work they are expected to do has changed and, very possibly, that the terms and conditions of their employment have altered.

Whilst all this is designed to increase the efficiency of a company it does mean that managing the human resources (employees) is becoming a more and more complex task. Ten years ago, if you worked in Personnel the chances are that other staff may have seen you as the office social worker or paperclip counter. These days more and more firms understand that if you don't get your people issues right you may find that nothing else works out.

Human resource management (often referred to as HRM) focuses on how businesses plan for the right number and type of staff; how they go about obtaining those staff; how they manage them; and how they get the best from them. Recent research by the Institute for Personnel & Development (the professional body for those working in human resource management) has shown that the ways people are managed have a greater effect on an organisation's performance than strategy, quality, manufacturing technology and research and development (R & D) put together.

It is important to distinguish between managing human resources, which is an activity everyone in an organisation is involved in to some extent, and the Human Resources Department and/or Personnel Department which exists in most large organisations. These departments employ specialists to provide advice and support to all employees on human resource matters. However, it is usually the responsibility of an individual manager to ensure that the employees in his or her area are able to do the jobs that have to be done. In small businesses, human resource management and personnel management are one and the same person, i.e. the proprietor.

The complexity of managing human resources means that many firms no longer try to do it all themselves. For instance, finding and keeping specialised staff is increasingly difficult, employment law is constantly changing and increasingly complex, and techniques for maintaining staff morale and providing high quality training are specialist skills in themselves.

Many organisations employ specialist firms to take on the more difficult areas. There are now about 4,500 recruitment agencies in the UK who not only take on the huge amount of work involved in sifting through applications but also have the specialist skills to ensure that they select the right people from fairly similar applications.

Figure 4.1 Getting extra help

| What's the difference between human resource management and personnel management?

Businesses have very different ideas of what human resource management involves. Some stick to the more traditional idea of personnel management, which is a function limited to recruiting, selecting, rewarding, managing and developing staff. This approach is linked to the idea that employees are costs of the business and have to be controlled and kept to a minimum.

Human resource management on the other hand regards employees as resources (as the name suggests). This encourages investment in training and development and other activities which increase the worth of these investments by making them better able and motivated to fulfil their job roles. This puts responsibility for employee relations firmly with

3

the management of a business whereas it has traditionally been regarded as the joint responsibility of management and the unions. It is a pro-active business-centred approach concerned with employee efficiency. Personnel management on the other hand is reactive, with its roots in the welfare function catering for staff needs as and when they arise.

There is disagreement about whether there is a difference between personnel management and human resource management and, if so, what that difference is. Typically the differences are defined as follows:

Table 4.1

Human Resource Management	Personnel Management
Employees are one of the most important assets of a business	Employees are one of the largest costs of a business
HRM is an integral part of a business's long-term planning and objective setting	Personnel management has a diverse role which is not a central strategic one
A business cannot perform well unless its human resources are managed effectively	Personnel management is important to business success
Employees must be committed to the success of the business	A business can succeed perfectly well without an actively supported workforce
It takes high quality staff to make high quality products	So long as systems and procedures are in place and high quality materials are used, products will be of a high quality even if the workforce is not excellent
Managers lead their teams	Managers manage their subordinates

In most organisations the Human Resource Department combines both approaches with an emphasis on human resource methodology.

CTIVITY

Here are two advertisements for specialists in human resource management or personnel. Which is for a human resource manager and which for a personnel manager? Which involves the broader range of responsibilities?

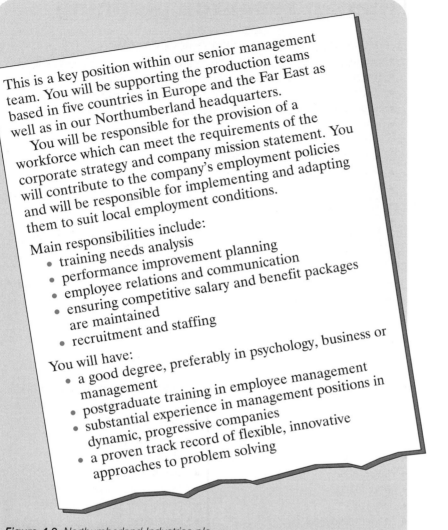

This is a key position within our senior management team. You will be supporting the production teams based in five countries in Europe and the Far East as well as in our Northumberland headquarters.

You will be responsible for the provision of a workforce which can meet the requirements of the corporate strategy and company mission statement. You will contribute to the company's employment policies and will be responsible for implementing and adapting them to suit local employment conditions.

Main responsibilities include:
- training needs analysis
- performance improvement planning
- employee relations and communication
- ensuring competitive salary and benefit packages are maintained
- recruitment and staffing

You will have:
- a good degree, preferably in psychology, business or management
- postgraduate training in employee management
- substantial experience in management positions in dynamic, progressive companies
- a proven track record of flexible, innovative approaches to problem solving

Figure 4.2 Northumberland Industries plc

We require an employee manager for our new factory in the West Midlands. You will be responsible for recruitment, employment procedures and policies, conditions of employment, employment-related administration and training. Applicants should possess a degree and have at least five years experience in a similar field. A recognised qualification in the employment field is essential.

Figure 4.3 West Midlands Engineering plc

Human resource planning

Human resource planning involves a strategy for the:
- recruitment
- retention
- utilisation
- improvement, and
- disposal

of the human resources of a business.

It needs to look at the following factors.
- What are the skills and abilities of the current workforce?
- What skills and abilities does the organisation need in the future?
- Where can the organisation find its future supply of labour?
- What are the future objectives of the business likely to be?
- How will the business obtain and manage its human resources to meet these objectives?

In order to plan its human resources effectively a business has to undertake considerable research. Table 4.2 shows the type of factors that companies take into account.

Table 4.2 The human resource planning process

What is happening now?	What do we expect to happen to the demand for products/services and therefore labour?
<ul><li>organisational objectives</li><li>analysis of staff numbers and age</li><li>wage rates</li><li>work loads</li><li>key skills</li><li>labour turnover</li><li>absenteeism</li></ul>	<ul><li>changing technology</li><li>sales forecasts</li><li>market research</li><li>new product development</li><li>managerial skills</li><li>wage rates</li><li>union agreements</li></ul>
What do we expect labour supply to be like in the future? Is there likely to be plenty or a shortage?	**All of these issues raise questions which the Human Resources Plan should cover. The plan will include:**
<ul><li>local unemployment/employment trends</li><li>local skills and availability</li><li>demographic changes</li><li>legislation</li><li>government training schemes</li><li>quality of local education, housing and transport</li><li>competition for workers</li></ul>	<ul><li>organisation development</li><li>training and management development</li><li>recruitment, redundancy and redeployment</li><li>appraisal and job evaluation</li><li>promotion prospects</li></ul>

Human resource planning is affected by internal and external factors. The external factors relate to circumstances which occur outside the business such as the economic situation and the local employment market. Usually the business has little control over these factors. All it can do is ensure that it knows the current situation and the likely trends over the next few years and understands how they affect the business's needs for employees and the availability of suitable people. Internal factors which need to be taken into account include growth and changes in the business, the age and skill profiles of existing staff, turnover, absenteeism and sickness rates. The business has more control over these factors and can develop policies and procedures to deal with them.

Analysing the external labour market

Businesses need to know whether they can find the right sort of people locally to employ. Decisions have to be made on whether to recruit relatively inexperienced staff at fairly low salaries and then invest in considerable training or recruit people who are sufficiently experienced and qualified. If so, there will be a higher salary bill but investment in staff training will be reduced and employees will be able to work efficiently and effectively from the start.

Businesses have to consider how much effort to put into attracting the right sort of people. If there are local skills shortages and many other businesses competing for the same people, more attractive packages of salaries, benefits and working conditions need to be considered. However, if there is an oversupply of properly qualified and experienced people, these packages can be reduced.

ACTIVITY

'Curl Up and Dye' is a family franchised hairdressing business with 12 branches in the East Midlands. Before deciding to open a new branch, a franchisee has to provide the company and the banks with a business plan which, among other things, shows:
- local employment trends
- local skills shortages
- competition for employees
- the availability of the right type of labour locally.

Select a small town close to where you live which doesn't have a branch of Curl Up and Dye. Write a report which could be used to apply for a franchise and which uses the four points above and draws conclusions about the local labour supply.

Have you checked out:

1 the local employment statistics collected by various government agencies, including Job Centres and the Office for National Statistics (www.ons.gov.uk)?

2 whether there is a high level of unemployment or is it difficult to recruit? What evidence have you collected from the local newspaper and the job centre? Have you asked at a local trendy hairdressers? How long does it take them to fill a vacancy? Why should your research not include hairdressers offering a 'short back and sides' or 'blue rinses'?

3 whether the local college runs hairdressing courses? How many of the students find jobs locally? Are they snapped up or does it take a while to find a job?

4 whether wages are low? If you were going to bid for a franchise, where would you place a job advertisement? What does this tell you?

5 how many trendy hairdressers there are in your area? How large is the local market? How many people are there in the 19–30 age range in the town? Contact your local economic development unit for information.

You should be able to think of lots more questions but many new businesses do not do this basic research and then find they cannot employ the right people at the right price.

Figure 4.4 *Hair we go!*

Dynamics of internal staffing

A business needs to understand the potential of its existing employees. It ought to ensure that it uses them to their maximum ability and that they work efficiently and effectively. It also needs to know when to recruit extra staff because of people getting new jobs, retiring or gaining promotion.

CASE STUDY

In a recent survey of annual labour turnover involving 706 organisations and 1.2 million workers, the Institute of Professional Development found that one in three craft and skilled manual workers had opted to move jobs. Among the accounting, legal and engineering professions turnover has risen by 8 per cent to 27 per cent. Forty-six per cent of the organisations surveyed found difficulty in recruiting professional staff, taking on average 14 weeks to fill a vacancy.

In reviewing the staffing situation a business needs to consider five issues.

Labour turnover

Most businesses collect statistics to monitor turnover by age, length of service, department, occupation and other relevant factors. Turnover rates are usually highest among the young, those whose skills are in demand and also new staff. High turnover rates are not a problem if there is a plentiful supply of suitable staff but it can be expensive if specialist skills and training are involved:

$$\text{Staff/labour turnover} = \frac{\text{Number of leavers during the year}}{\text{Average number of people employed during the year}} \times 100$$

This is a fairly rough indicator of performance since it tells you very little about what is happening. For example, a 50 per cent turnover may mean that half the workforce left during the year or 10 per cent were replaced five times each. To cope with this, most organisations use the labour stability index.

$$\text{Labour stability index} = \frac{\text{No. of employees with one or more years service}}{\text{No. of people employed at the beginning of the year}} \times 100$$

This tells us how many people have been in the business for a least one year. In many organisations the most valued personnel are those who have been employed for several years. Low turnover amongst these staff is therefore a critical indicator.

ACTIVITY

Using an organisation you know, work out the percentage staff turnover and the labour stability index. Try to calculate these for your school or college. What are the effects of a high level of staff turnover in a school or college?

The costs associated with labour turnover include:
- loss of production while the vacancy is unfilled
- loss of production during training
- cost of recruitment and subsequent training
- low morale
- cost of mistakes by new employees
- payment of overtime until replacement workers can be recruited.

It is the role of the Human Resources Manager to ensure that excessively high turnover rates are watched carefully and strategies put in place to reduce them. This may include one or more of the following:
- review of employee selection, recruitment, induction and training
- improving working conditions including pay and other benefits
- improving morale and team culture
- job enrichment to improve job satisfaction
- improving promotion prospects.

Clearly, much of this is obvious but may be outside the control of the HRM department, particularly if the company is subject to budget constraints and part of the problem has been caused by corporate downsizing. Many firms have faced a staffing situation of large numbers of inexperienced young workers as a result of restructuring.

Downsizing, page 14

Sickness rates

This is a significant cost for organisations. Many public sector organisations have particular problems in this field as do employers where jobs are mundane and boring. Businesses where morale is low may also suffer high sickness rates. It is worth calculating the frequency rate (FR) which shows the average number of spells of absence per employee:

$$FR = \frac{\text{No. of spells of absence per time period}}{\text{No. of employees in the time period}} \times 100$$

Employers often complain that workers treat sick days as additional holidays. Whenever workers are off sick other employees have to cover for them or temporary staff have to be employed. The former usually attract overtime payments and the latter involve additional costs of using agency staff.

Absenteeism can be measured. Measuring the extent of the problem is often the first stage of controlling absence. Businesses frequently publish their absenteeism rates for a given time period. The lost time rate (LTR) shows the percentage of total time lost due to absence from all causes in a given time period. It is calculated as:

$$LTR = \frac{\text{Total absence in a given time period}}{\text{Possible total available in time period}} \times 100$$

For example, if the total absences are 300 hours out of a possible 12,000 hours, lost time is 2.5 per cent.

Age, skills and training

Organisations carry out regular analyses of their skill needs using a skills audit. These audits try to establish what skills exist and what will be needed in the future. The audit of the company's needs is often completed using information from line managers.

Similarly, most HRM departments draw up an age profile to check whether there might be problems because the age profile is too high or too low. In the former it can lead to recruitment difficulties, particularly if all the experienced staff retire in quick succession. If all the staff are young the department or company may suffer from a lack of experience leading to a fall in output. A spread of ages is the most desirable although it very much depends on the organisation.

Succession

Grooming successors for supervisory and management posts is a good idea and can cut costs of recruitment. This approach is sometimes viewed with suspicion by the present postholder. Who can blame them? However, good managers try to ensure that if and when they move on or retire someone who is trained and knows what they are doing is waiting in the wings. This is an example of good managers being able to share their experiences and not feeling threatened by potential successors. This is probably easier said than done in a climate where redundancy, downsizing and delayering of middle management positions lead to feelings of insecurity and an unwillingness to share knowledge and skills.

❙ You can't get the staff these days!

Recruitment is about getting the right people for the right job at the right time. It involves deciding what staff the organisation needs, advertising to get the right sort of people to apply and choosing from those applicants the ones best suited to the jobs.

 Staff appraisal, page 67

Figure 4.5 Do these people exist?

Can you crack a smile and look sad at the same time?

Walk the plank with a bucket of water balanced on your head?

Our superb training will develop your skills to the maximum.
As a clown in our travelling circuses you will get plenty of opportunity to move on. In fact we're looking forward to it!
We have vacancies for several clown troupes in circuses around the globe. So if you are fit and healthy and fancy the travelling, why not contact us on 01279 814173
or email smile@circ.com

As an equal opportunities employer we are pleased to receive applications from men and women members of ethnic communities and people with disabilities

---

This is one of the most vital decisions an organisation can make. If you recruit the wrong person it can be very difficult to get rid of them. In the meantime you can be stuck with someone who cannot or will not perform to the right level. In the worst situations this leads to the business losing money. For instance, a receptionist who cannot handle the latest equipment properly may not be able to pass on important sales enquiries.

Later in this book you will see how successful recruitment involves careful consideration of the job being created and the type of person who will be able to do this job. Usually the people who know best what is required are the people who are doing that type of job already or know which role(s) are necessary to complement their team. Their participation in the recruitment process is essential. It is also worth listening to the views of other team members since they are already doing the job and are aware of the attributes and complementary skills needed to create a complete team.

ⒸASE STUDY

Well qualified but terrible worker

It is increasingly becoming obvious that paper qualifications and experience do not necessarily mean someone has the ability to do the job. Many good people with potential are passed over by conventional recruitment methods. Why should a firm take on a 19-year-old with a criminal record and no qualifications rather than someone who has NVQs and is a safe bet? Many companies do not consider carefully enough the role of the new employee or their ability to learn.

ⒸASE STUDY

Previous employment: Army driver
Experience: refuelling combat aircraft in Gulf War
Post advertised: staff job in a team of Shell drivers handling many non-core deliveries outside the retail network covering 45 million kilometres each year carrying 8 billion litres of highly flammable cargo.

Figure 4.6 *John Bannister*

Figure 4.7 Making sure we get the right person

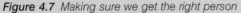

Training is critical since employees need to be much more than drivers. They need the ability to self manage, solve problems, load vehicles safely, drive safely and complete each delivery not only safely but in a way that satisfies the client, since they are Shell's most frequent point of contact with customers.

After passing the various Shell aptitude tests as well as a driving test, John went back to the classroom for a week's theoretical training before setting foot in a vehicle. Training lasted about four weeks and included customer service, quality systems, product knowledge, emergency procedures, first aid and protective training. But that wasn't the end of it. For all Shell drivers training is a continuing feature of their working lives. The company runs regular refresher courses for their drivers who are certified against the European Standard for the transport of hazardous goods by road – and driver training of a more general nature for qualifications such as the Institute of Advanced Motorists advanced driving test, defensive driving technique, etc. In addition, non-driving training covers manual handling together with regular briefings on environmental issues.

Aptitude tests, pages 32 and 33

Recruitment is not just about whether someone has the qualifications to do the job but whether are they adaptable, flexible and willing to learn. Companies spend large sums of money attempting to get the mix right.

| All change

It is increasingly recognised that the only certain thing about managing a business today is that change will occur continually. Thirty or forty years ago most organisations would expect very little change in their circumstances unless they deliberately sought it. As a result business planning was relatively easy and managing change was not regarded as a key management function.

Any change in the way an organisation performs inevitably has human resource implications and it is the role of the Human Resource Manager to anticipate, plan for and implement these changes. The types of changes that affect a business's human resource requirements include the following.

Changes in the business's size

Businesses make plans which forecast short- and long-term changes in the level of sales. As sales increase the business may have to employ more staff. Initially this is likely to be on the production side (or those providing the service in the service sector, e.g. the accountants in an accountancy firm). If sales increase further there will be a greater need for sales staff, office staff and managers. The human resource manager works with managers from the various departments to plan how many staff are needed, when new staff will be required and what skills and experiences they will need to have.

Similar decisions have to be made when businesses decrease in size. As sales decline, the business will have more labour than it requires. Often this decrease is not properly anticipated and the changes in staffing are unplanned and sudden. Alternatively a company may plan to reduce its overall size even when sales are growing because the management has identified inefficiencies which can be solved by downsizing, delayering and, therefore, making redundancies.

Shifts in products or markets

These can affect the type of staff that a company needs. Over the last ten years, competition in many products has focused not on the physical product itself but on the after-sales service attached to it. As a result many manufacturers have had to employ people who can provide the after-sales service as well as those who make the actual product. This may involve creating new jobs such as telephone customer care staff or it may require extensive retraining of existing staff.

For example, Hoover now train their maintenance staff to provide advice on contracts, replacement machines and other factors and all in a customer-friendly fashion. Hoover wants its ex-maintenance engineers not just to mend your machine but to provide a service.

Key terms

Downsizing – reducing the number of employees often through redundancy or outsourcing.
Delayering – the removal of one or more layers of management. This often involves dismissing middle managers.
Outsourcing – where work previously completed by a business is contracted out to another company. This has particularly affected business services such as IT provision, catering, and cleaning.
Multi skilling – where workers can do most of the jobs in their department rather than just one or two tasks.

The introduction of new technology

This leads to several different types of changes in human resource requirements. In some production plants there has been a reduction in the number of staff though the remaining people are much better qualified and are multi-skilled. Technology has not only reduced the number of staff but has deskilled those still employed as more sophisticated machinery replaces skilled people while the more unskilled work has often remained. Office workers have also had to be retrained to cope with the introduction of computer systems and then have their skills constantly updated as new software packages are introduced.

New regulations, legislation or government policies

These are changes over which a business rarely has any influence. They are often difficult to predict. New requirements over health and safety at work can reduce, for instance, the number of hours a driver may be at the wheel without a break. A company may therefore have to employ more people to shift the same amount of goods. Similarly the introduction of the minimum wage in 1999 has increased businesses' costs.

The economic situation

If the government changes its fiscal (taxation) policy, for instance by deciding to reduce levels of income tax, this can increase consumers' disposable income and lead to an increase in demand for a company's products. If the Monetary Policy Committee of the Bank of England increases interest rates, this may lead to a fall in consumer demand. Similarly, changes in the European or world economy can affect demand; an example is the collapse of the Asian economy in the late 1990s.

Ⓒ ASE STUDY

How the devaluation of the Thai baht lost Graham Jones his job

When the value of Thailand's currency fell, Graham Jones didn't notice or care. But within 15 months he was on the dole. The Asian crisis in 1998 had far-reaching effects on many businesses.

The devaluation

In 1997 several property companies in Thailand collapsed, leaving investors with bad debts and a surplus of unwanted properties. This oversupply of office properties led to a fall in property prices. This affected overseas investors' views of the Thai economy and speculators sold Thailand's currency (the baht). As the value of the baht fell, Thailand's exports became cheaper, making it harder for neighbouring countries to compete.

Figure 4.8 *The beginning of the end*

The big shutdown

On 31 July 1998, managers at Siemens, the German electronics company, called in workers at the semi-conductor group on North Tyneside and said they would be sacked. The company was not able to compete with cheap exports from the Far East.

The cleaners

One third of the workers at Mitie, a cleaning company, could not be redeployed following the loss of the Siemens contract.

The hotel – Stakis

Craig Dent didn't sleep the night he heard about Siemens. He would not only be affected by the loss of business from the German executives but also by the loss of suppliers and contractors like Mitie. The hotel had to find other customers, especially other sales representatives and family groups. The receptionist quickly noticed that families and sales reps came in their own cars and didn't use taxis.

The taxi firm – Foxhunters

Trade had been brisk. Foxhunters had a contract to run executives to and from the Stakis, the airport, and the factory, etc. Tips were good and the business was a 'little gold mine'. Drivers suddenly had no work. They lounged in the pool room waiting for fares and complained about the broken pinball machine, the coffee machine and much else. Most of them were earning between £100 and £200 per week less. Cabbies like Lee began to delay upgrading their cars and a number had to make economies such as not going to the pub.

The public bar – Cameron's

Takings plunged £600 per week when regulars like Lee began cutting down on their visits. Robert Lavey, the landlord, heard the same story from many other regulars. He had to let two of his four staff go.

Graham Jones – the barman

He wasn't surprised when he was fired. Trade was very slow and he knew it couldn't go on. The ripples from Thailand had turned into a wave and washed away his job. There were thousands like him throughout the country.

In making changes to the workforce, businesses aim to meet predictable changes in demand for staff but also retain enough flexibility to respond to future unforeseen changes. Companies can make their workforces more flexible by the following methods.

Flexible contracts, page 52

Employing more part-time employees

PART-TIME SALES ASSISTANT

Enthusiastic, adaptable, reliable part-timer required to join hardworking team in busy Regent Street jewellers.
Please apply to:
Box 71849
Hertfordshire Messenger
New Albany Street
Hertford
HT1 8BR

CELICON AGROCHEMICALS
Analytical Chemist required, to work 1,195 hours per annum.
£7.40 per hour.
Apply to:
Abby Anderson
Human Resource Manager
21 Denby Road
Stafford ST7 8QZ

e-mail A.Anderson@zen.com

Telephones R Us

A career with our sales team. You will be responsible for selling our services to customers in their homes. You will work part time, mainly in the afternoons and evenings. You will not accept earnings of less than £15,000 p.a. plus a mileage allowance and regular incentives. You need to be familiar with the internet, and have a car and a full driving licence.
Please telephone us on 0800 979797, or send a CV to Brandon Keep, Chesney House, Northwich, Cheshire, or e-mail to TelephonesRUs@aol.com quoting ref. CER 791876.

Figure 4.9 Changing patterns of work

Over half of the major supermarkets' workforces are part-time. This allows them to provide sufficient staff in the stores at peak times without having to pay all their staff for the periods when there is less demand.

Employing people on temporary contracts

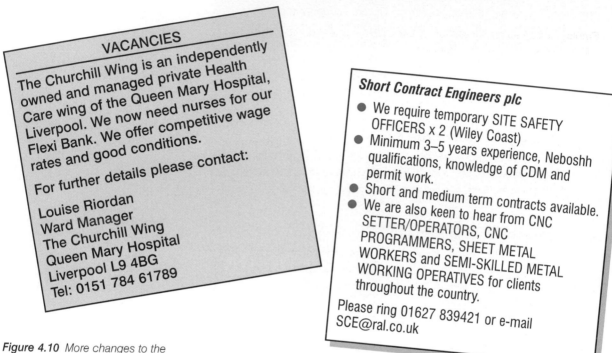

VACANCIES

The Churchill Wing is an independently owned and managed private Health Care wing of the Queen Mary Hospital, Liverpool. We now need nurses for our Flexi Bank. We offer competitive wage rates and good conditions.

For further details please contact:

Louise Riordan
Ward Manager
The Churchill Wing
Queen Mary Hospital
Liverpool L9 4BG
Tel: 0151 784 61789

Short Contract Engineers plc
● We require temporary SITE SAFETY OFFICERS x 2 (Wiley Coast)
● Minimum 3–5 years experience, Neboshh qualifications, knowledge of CDM and permit work.
● Short and medium term contracts available.
● We are also keen to hear from CNC SETTER/OPERATORS, CNC PROGRAMMERS, SHEET METAL WORKERS and SEMI-SKILLED METAL WORKING OPERATIVES for clients throughout the country.

Please ring 01627 839421 or e-mail SCE@ral.co.uk

Figure 4.10 *More changes to the nature of work*

This may be seasonal. The Post Office employs many temporary staff around Christmas to cope with the unusually large amounts of mail. For other businesses, temporary staff may be hired to cover for people who are ill or on holiday. The NHS uses nurse banks so that part-time workers registered with them can be called in to work at short notice.

Contract workers
These people are often self-employed and are hired by a business for a fixed length of time to do a particular job. Many computer specialists and engineers have this type of contract.

Annualised hours
Annualised hours systems contract employees to work a given number of hours over a twelve-month period. The business is then able to vary the amount worked in any week (between agreed minima and maxima) to respond to demand.

CASE STUDY

Agrochemical manufacturers and ice cream manufacturers may not seem to have much in common. But both experience seasonal peaks in demand. If staff were employed for a regular 40 hours per week they would be standing around with very little to do for some of the year. However, when demand peaks they have to work overtime. Employers can either lay staff off at slack time and re-employ them later or have annual hours contracts.

Figure 4.11 Could you eat more ice cream in the winter please?

Gerry works for a large ice cream manufacturer. 'I used to work say 30 hours per week during the winter and 50 hours per week during the summer. I would be laid off over the winter for some of the time, making my income very uncertain. Under the new arrangements I work 1,670 hours per year but I do not get overtime unless I work more than this. My income is stable and regular.'

Zero hours contracts

These are used in the retail trade and fast-food restaurants. Staff have contracts for zero hours which ensures they are available for work but there is no guarantee of employment. Staff are expected to be available for work at short notice to meet unforeseen absences or changes in demand. Staff on these contracts are only paid when they work.

It is important that changes in the workforce be carefully planned since they are expensive and not easy to implement. The costs of making the changes include the time and money spent on recruiting, training and making people redundant, as well as the cost of making mistakes. If insufficient staff are available, a company may not be able to produce enough to meet the demand for its products. If staff are not trained in appropriate work skills, they may make errors, work inefficiently or damage machinery.

The difficulties in implementing changes with the workforce occur for a number of reasons:

- legislation protects the rights of employees
- many people have an inherent resistance to change; the human resource manager has to identify strategies for overcoming this resistance
- employees' motivation.

Is your organisation healthy?

Sometimes employees' actions stifle initiative, prevent change and create an unhealthy climate which leads to resistance to change. The following 'rules' ensure change is limited!

1 Regard any new idea from below with suspicion.

2 Insist that those who need your approval go through several layers of management to get your signature.

3 Ask departments and individuals to challenge and criticise each other's proposals. Then managers can pick the survivors.

4 Express your criticism freely and withhold your praise. This keeps people on their toes. Let them know they can be fired at any time.

5 Treat problems as signs of failure and discourage people from letting you know when something isn't working.

6 Control everything carefully, making sure people count everything that can be counted frequently.

7 Make decisions to reorganise and change policies in secret and spring them on people suddenly. This keeps people on their toes.

8 Make sure that any request for information is fully justified and that it isn't distributed freely.

9 Assign to lower-level managers responsibility for layoffs and cutbacks.

10 Above all, never forget that those at the top already know everything there is to know about the business.

(Taken from Kanter, *The Change Masks: Corporate Entrepreneurs at Work*, Allen and Unwin 1983)

Note!

One of the major responsibilities of any organisation is to make sure that it has the right people in the right jobs at the right time. There are three stages in this process:

- determining what the business needs
- recruiting a range of suitable applicants for the post
- selecting the right person.

Change causes uncertainty. People fear for their jobs. Change must be handled in such a way that it creates minimum disruption to the workforce and is seen by those involved and/or remaining as of positive benefit to the company and their contribution to it.

Recruitment and selection

If an organisation is to achieve its objectives, having the right people working for it is a critical factor for success.

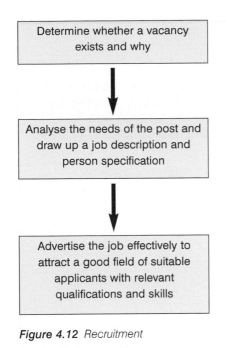

Determine whether a vacancy exists and why

↓

Analyse the needs of the post and draw up a job description and person specification

↓

Advertise the job effectively to attract a good field of suitable applicants with relevant qualifications and skills

Figure 4.12 *Recruitment*

Draw up a shortlist from the applicants by matching their applications with the job description and person specification

↓

Select a candidate for the post through interviews and/or aptitude tests

↓

Offer the job to the successful candidate. Draw up a contract of employment

↓

Provide induction to new employee

↓

Develop the skills and abilities of staff throughout their employment

Figure 4.13 *Selection and one step beyond*

Does the vacancy exist?

Just because someone leaves an organisation doesn't necessarily mean that they need to be replaced or that the job role now requires identical skills to those of the person who has left. Similarly, just because a team requests more staff does not necessarily mean that an appointment can be justified.

Why has the vacancy arisen?

Vacancies arise for several reasons.

Growth of the business

After at least a decade of downsizing, streamlining and general cost cutting, the millennium saw companies putting growth back on the agenda. Increasing returns on investment and sales revenue are creating new job opportunities.

Questions to ask:

- Does the organisation need a replacement or could the responsibilities be reallocated to other staff?

- Does the team/organisation need extra staff or would a redefinition of everyone's job roles provide the cover without incurring additional costs or work overload?

- Should the job role be redefined so that a new employee's contribution would be more effective and efficient?

- Can the business afford to fill the vacancy?

FEEST

MANUFACTURING MANAGEMENT
Excellent Benefits and Relocation Package

We think we are the success story among chilled food manufacturers. We have launched over 100 new products in the last year alone. To continue this growth we need the best people. We are looking for high quality production professionals who are forward thinking and up to date in their approach.

If you would like to work in East Anglia in a pressurised, challenging and very dynamic environment, why not send details of your career and current renumeration to our retained recruitment advisers at the address below, quoting reference AJL 71.

Recruitment International
Ironduke Way
Waterlooville
Hants PS3 9LM

Email: contact@recruitment.co.uk
Tel: 01376 901396
Fax: 01376 902395

Figure 4.14 *More jobs please!*

Changing job roles

As new technology is introduced, new markets are developed. Consequently job roles need to be redefined and new ones added.

CASE STUDY

Figure 4.15 *First Direct*

Whilst banks like National Westminster, Barclays and HSBC are busy shedding clerical and administrative staff from their branch and central networks, tele-banking leader First Direct is expanding its workforce and the size of its purpose-built headquarters. Its job roles are specified in competences like learning skills, attitude and ability to improve one's own performance rather than the possession of previous branch banking experience. This is because new recruits can develop banking skills through training.

Resignation and retirement

All organisations lose staff as a result of resignation and retirement. Some go to other companies or organisations because they are unhappy or want a change or a new challenge. Some will retire at 60 or 65 whilst others take early retirement. Companies need to track the numbers who leave by calculating their staff turnover rate.

 Staff turnover rate, page 9

They also need to be aware of what frontline employees say about them. Is it going to be easy to attract the kind of people you want to replace those leaving? It also begs the question 'What is morale like?' and how does the company know?

Promotion

Job opportunities frequently arise because of the promotion of the current postholder either to another organisation or within the business itself.

CASE STUDY

Danes Retail Foods Ltd

The company has the following structure:

```
┌─────────────────────────┐
│   Production manager     │
└─────────────────────────┘
             │
┌─────────────────────────┐
│       Supervisor         │
└─────────────────────────┘
             │
┌─────────────────────────┐
│      Charge hands        │
└─────────────────────────┘
             │
┌─────────────────────────┐
│      Floor workers       │
└─────────────────────────┘
```

Figure 4.16 *Danes Retail Foods Ltd*

The Production Manager recently left to join a competing company and Danes, having established the need for the role, decided to recruit a replacement. The job was advertised internally and in the local paper. A supervisor in the quality control department was promoted and this then created a promotional opportunity at supervisor level. The company then decided to recruit from the charge hands and subsequently upgrade a floor worker. A vacancy then arose for a floor worker, which was advertised in the local paper.

A job description
This states, broadly, what the purpose, duties and responsibilities of the job will be. It normally consists of:

- **job title**
- **purpose of the job**
- **main tasks to be done**
- **how the postholder fits into the business's organisational structure and to whom he/she will be accountable. It will also state his/her staffing responsibilities**
- **the limits of his/her authority**
- **the resources that are available and the budget responsibilities if this is appropriate**
- **targets and goals to be achieved and how performance will be assessed**
- **special requirements – including whether the job involves shift work.**

What does the organisation need?

Before advertising a job vacancy, it is important to have a clear view about the competences, qualities and qualifications the role requires. In other words, a description of the job that needs doing.

Describing the job

Job descriptions are useful for ensuring that employees do the job for which they were taken on. They also enable managers to insist that anything within the job description is done by the employee. However, too rigid job descriptions in a rapidly changing environment can stifle learning and creativity. Where roles are too closely defined, employees may spend the whole day doing the same standard procedures over and over. Such tight constraints do not leave enough room for businesses to benefit from individuals using their experience or learning to improve performance. Similarly, employees may refuse to do something that is not in their job description. This highlights the need for managers to regularly review job descriptions to ensure they are still relevant and match the needs of the organisation. In some organisations this is done as part of the annual performance review of each employee.

CASE STUDY

Job description

Nursery Nurse

Purpose of Post
a To provide a high standard of physical, emotional, social and intellectual care for children placed in the Nursery.
b To give support to other staff within the Nursery.
c To implement the daily routine in the base room.

Responsible to
The Nursery Manager

Duties and Responsibilities
1 Operating, in conjunction with other staff, a programme of activities suitable to the age range of children in your area
2 Keeping a proper record of achievement file on your children for parents/guardians
3 Working with parents/guardians of special needs children to provide full integration into the Nursery
4 Supporting all staff and participating in the staff team
5 Liaising with and supporting parents/guardians and other family members
6 Being involved in all out of working hours activities, e.g. training, staff meetings, parents evenings, summer fair, Christmas party, etc
7 Working flexibly within the practices of the Nursery. Being prepared to help where needed, including undertaking certain domestic jobs within the Nursery, e.g. preparation of snack meals, cleaning equipment, etc
8 Working alongside the Manager and staff team to ensure that the philosophy behind the Nursery is implemented
9 Recording accidents in the accident book and ensuring that the Manager has initialled the report before the parent/guardian receives it
10 Looking upon the Nursery as a 'whole' where your contribution can be best utilised and being constantly aware of the needs of children
11 Ensuring each child is collected by someone who is known to Nursery staff and who is over the age of 18
12 Respecting the confidentiality of information received
13 Developing your role within the team especially as a key worker
14 Carrying out specific childcare tasks:
  • Preparing and completing activities to suit the child's stage of development
  • Ensuring that mealtimes are a pleasant social gathering
  • Washing and changing children as required
  • Providing comfort and warmth to a poorly child
15 Ensuring the provision of a high quality environment to meet the needs of individual children, whatever their culture or religious background or stage of development
16 Being aware of the good reputation of the Nursery and upholding its standards at all times.

It will be very difficult to get the right person if you are not clear about the type of person needed. Companies therefore carry out an analysis of the job, which involves deciding upon:

- the purpose of the role
- the tasks to be performed
- who the person is accountable to and for what
- performance criteria which form the basis for review and appraisal; this enables the organisation to assess whether the person is performing to the required standards
- the competences required for the post, such as knowledge and skills
- the responsibilities of the post
- the structure of the organisation and the position of the postholder within it
- environmental factors such as hygiene and health and safety requirements
- factors that will motivate workers
- the training requirements of the postholder.

Job analysis is necessary so that:

- the rate of pay can be established
- a training programme can be devised
- efficient and effective recruitment can occur.

Describing the person needed to fill the vacancy

After the analysis described above has been done, a person specification is drawn up. This lists the essential and desirable skills which applicants need, such as

- knowledge
- intelligence
- general skills
- specialist skills
- previous experience
- academic and job related qualifications
- age
- physical characteristics
- personality.

Many organisations base their person specifications loosely on systems such as those shown in the following tables.

Table 4.3 *Rodgers 7-point plan*

Physical characteristics	Health, physique, appearance, bearing and energy
Attainment	Education, qualifications, experience
Intelligence	Thinking and mental skills, intellectual skills
Special aptitudes	Mechanical, manual dexterity, ability to use words/numbers
Interests	Intellectual, practical, physical, artistic, social
Disposition	Acceptability, influence over others, steadiness, dependability, self-reliance
Circumstances	Domestic/family

Table 4.4 *Munro-Fraser 5-fold grading system*

Impact on others	Physical make up, appearance, bearing, manner and speech
Acquired qualifications	Education, training and work experience
Innate (natural) abilities	Natural quickness of comprehension, ability to learn
Motivation	The kind of goals set by a person, consistency and determination to succeed
Adjustment	Emotional stability, ability to withstand stress, ability to get on with people

St. Bart's

St. Bart's House Day Nursery and Pre School
17 Dover Road, Sandwich CT13 0BS
Phone/fax: 01304 621911

NURSERY NURSE

Personnel Specification

Attributes	Criterion Number	Criteria	How Identified	Rank
Relevant Experience	1	2 years post qualifying experience in a day-care setting	Application/Interview	C-Advantageous
	2	Experience working with young children	Application/Interview	A-Essential
	3	Knowledge of key worker systems and record keeping	Interview	B-Desirable
Education and Training	4	NNEB Diploma or equivalent	Application	A-Essential
	5	Recent First Aid qualification	Application	C-Advantageous
	6	Basic Food Hygiene Certificate	Application	C-Advantageous
	7	Other related training	Application/Interview	C-Advantageous
General and Special Knowledge	8	Knowledge of The Children Act	Interview	B-Desirable
	9	Knowledge of the Desirable Learning Outcomes/Early Learning Goals	Interview	B-Desirable
	10	Knowledge of child development	Interview	A-Essential
Skills and Abilities	11	Ability to communicate well with adults and children	Interview	A-Essential
	12	Ability to work as part of a team	Interview	B-Desirable
	13	Ability to write legibly and to have good presentation skills	Application/Interview	B-Desirable
	14	Computer literate	Application/Interview	C-Advantageous
	15	Good organisational skills	Interview	C-Advantageous
	16	Creative ability	Interview	B-Desirable
Additional Factors	17	Understanding of Equal Opportunities	Interview	B-Desirable
	18	Awareness of Health and Safety and practical hygiene issues	Interview	B-Desirable
	19	Ability to take on a responsibility role	Application/Interview	C-Advantageous

Figure 4.17 *Nursery nurse – Person specification*

Getting the right applicants

When to advertise

Businesses need to plan when they advertise to ensure that they maximise the number of suitable applicants. They need to take account of:

- local labour market conditions
- local holidays when factories shut and most families take their annual holidays
- national holidays such as Christmas and New Year when the number of people who see and respond to advertisements is reduced
- resignation dates
- journal publication dates
- newspaper publication dates, for example many local or weekly papers have a Tuesday 12.00 deadline for Friday publication.

Where should you advertise?

The next stage is to attract the right people to apply for the job. Business organisations may use the following recruitment methods.

Internal advertisements

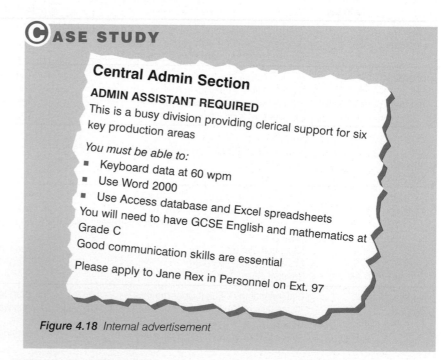

CASE STUDY

Central Admin Section

ADMIN ASSISTANT REQUIRED

This is a busy division providing clerical support for six key production areas

You must be able to:
- Keyboard data at 60 wpm
- Use Word 2000
- Use Access database and Excel spreadsheets

You will need to have GCSE English and mathematics at Grade C

Good communication skills are essential

Please apply to Jane Rex in Personnel on Ext. 97

Figure 4.18 *Internal advertisement*

You will notice that this advertisement has an informal feel.

External advertisements through newspapers, magazines, professional journals, etc

ⒸASE STUDY

ALPHA TELECOM

Customer Care Agents, Battersea (Shift Work)   **£12,500 + Overtime**

ALPHA TELECOM is a next-generation communications company which enables business and residential callers to substantially reduce costs of national, mobile and international telephone calls.

You will be responsible for providing an efficient and professional service to our customers.

As a Customer Care Agent you will need a minimum of 12 months experience in a customer care environment. You will be flexible and have a friendly and focused approach. A basic working knowledge of computers is essential as is a willingness to learn and grow with the company.

Call our recruitment hotline on 0208 262 0130

OFFICE SERVICES   **Central London**

MTV Networks Europe needs little introduction – we are the recognised name at the forefront of music television. We are now offering a rare opportunity to play a part in an exciting, innovative and creative environment, providing a range of vital administrative functions within Office Services.

Office Services Co-ordinator

You'll play a central role within the department, assisting the Head of Office Services and co-ordinating a range of functions. These will include liaising with suppliers, helping with contract tenders, monitoring performance and ensuring our records are accurate. Experience in an administrative or office role is required.

Office Services Assistant

You will provide administrative support to the Head of Office Services and her team. Typing, filing, dealing with telephone enquiries and arranging appointments will all be part of your brief. Knowledge of Excel, Powerpoint and JDEdwards is preferred.

Interested? Please send your CV and covering letter to Andrea Pritchard, MTV Networks Europe, UK House, 180 Oxford Street, London W1N 0DS by 17 November.

Key terms

Networking – when you hear of jobs through contacts at work, friends or family.

Headhunting – when a consultancy company is commissioned to look for the best person to fill the job. This approach is often used for senior positions where the organisation may not, for a variety of reasons, wish to reveal that it is trying to recruit.

CV or curriculum vitae, page 37

Foreign Exchange

Cashiers   **Waterloo International**

If you're over 19, with some knowledge of French and have good customer service skills, then International Currency Exchange could have just the job for you, based at our prestigious Waterloo International branch.

You will be providing a fast, friendly foreign exchange service to international customers from around the world. Numerate and accurate, you'll be cool under pressure and ideally have a banking/retail background or cash handling skills. Experience of working with foreign currency would be an added advantage and you must be prepared to work a shift pattern between the hours of 6 am and 11 pm.

To apply, please send your CV with covering letter, including your current salary details to:

Gillian Plant
Personnel Manager
International Currency Exchange Ltd
Albany Courtyard, 47-48 Piccadilly
London W1V 0LR

The Internet

ⒸASE STUDY

Net gains

Many people looking for jobs use the Internet to increase their chances of getting their CV in front of the right people. Switched-on job seekers will use everything available to them. Going online gives key information about the companies you'd like to work for, will introduce you to recruitment agencies and offer tips on interviews. For example, job-hunting nurses can now do so without traipsing around hospitals and recruitment agencies. Try www.nurse.co.uk for hundreds of nursing jobs with online application forms.

Other methods

Other avenues of recruitment include:
- private employment agencies such as Angels, Manpower
- government-run Job Centres

- FE colleges, schools and universities as well as training establishments
- phone calls or letters to companies enquiring about vacancies.

Figure 4.19 Government Job Centre

Other considerations

The method used depends on the type of job, its status and whether it is very specialised or not and, of course, cost. As a general rule, unskilled and semi-skilled jobs as well as manual work tend to be advertised locally, whereas management and senior posts tend to be advertised nationally and/or through agencies. Jobs requiring specialist skills such as chemists, social workers, teachers and managers are usually advertised in specialist journals. When advertising vacancies, companies have to take account of the laws governing recruitment and selection.

 Equal opportunities legislation, pages 76–78

Effective selection

Critical to the recruitment process is selecting candidates for shortlisting for final interviewing. Companies usually require people interested in the vacant position to send in a curriculum vitae and/or complete an application form.

These are used to select candidates for interview. This is called a shortlist. Sometimes for higher level and specialist jobs companies draw up a long-list. There is then a process which involves two or three interviews, tests, etc from which a shortlist is compiled. Most small businesses carry out the whole process themselves.

Steps which companies consider in deciding how to select candidates include the following.

 Curriculum vitae, pages 36–37

 Application form, page 38

Targeting

Headhunters may be used to find particular individuals for the job. This method is widely used in the City of London for brokers, dealers, chief executives, etc. It is also used when companies are recruiting for overseas posts or for senior posts which have to be kept secret until the final selection is made.

Testing

Testing entails an attempt to discover a person's potential or problems, using psychometric approaches. Many businesses incorporate real work into the interview process and use tests, such as 'in-tray' exercises. For example, organisations may give candidates a selection of memos and letters to answer and ask them to put the tasks in order according to their importance. Which letter, memo or problem will you deal with first, which one next? You will probably also have a time limit set for the exercise. This assesses your ability to set priorities and work to deadlines. Unsuccessful candidates usually deal with the problem at the top of the pile rather than reading through the whole exercise to see which tasks are the most important and doing those first. Potential employees in call centres are usually given a series of phone calls to deal with to check their telephone manner and their ability to keep calm.

Testimonials

These are references written and given to the employee. They are usually headed 'To whom it may concern'. Job seekers then copy them and send them with their CV. They are not very widely used as they can easily be forged and tend to be written in very vague language.

References

All organisations ask for references though they are difficult to interpret. A referee may provide a glowing reference to get rid of someone and only a foolish applicant would cite a referee they know would not be supportive. Most prospective employers insist on contacting current employers to ask for a written reference and they may well follow it up with a phone call. Referees are frequently willing to give a more frank assessment of the candidate over the phone than in writing.

A bit of light assessment

Over the last twenty years there has been increased use of all types of tests. These are designed to assess how good people are at certain things and are used to predict a candidate's future performance. Tests are sometimes carried out to reduce a 'long list' to a shortlist. They are also used at the shortlist stage. Much depends on the company and how important it views such tests. A recent analysis of recruitment methods by the Institute of Personnel & Development found that 61 per cent of firms used aptitude tests, 43 per cent used personality questionnaires and 30 per cent evaluated potential staff at assessment centres. Professional and managerial staff are particularly likely to be put through a wide range of processes before reaching the final interview.

There are several different types of tests.

Psychometric tests

These are designed to measure a candidate's mental abilities. They try to establish candidates' aptitude or ability for certain types of work and to measure their levels of competence in work related skills. They may also include 'personality tests' designed to measure personality traits which an employer thinks are important for the job. It may be important for the organisation to know whether an applicant stays calm but alert in certain conditions, whether he or she is adaptable and likes change or whether he or she prefers stability. To make these tests useful they need to be fair, consistent and reliable. They should be:

- taken under standardised conditions with strictly applied time limits
- carried out by someone who is trained in their use and has a qualification which ensures they are competent
- objectively marked – usually through a computer or an electronic scanning machine.

Such selection tests will have been through rigorous checking before being used. They are usually used as part of a wider set of selection procedures including CV, application forms and interviews.

Some posts may require a whole day at an 'assessment centre'. There may be in-tray exercises, or group decision-making or problem-solving exercises. These test organisational skills, planning abilities and how effectively the candidates function in teams.

Since selection and recruitment are costly and time-consuming processes, tests are frequently used to filter out unsuitable candidates. This can be very useful for organisations with several hundred applications for each vacancy.

ⒸASE STUDY

Assessment, assessment, assessment

Many popular employers, such as multinationals and companies in expanding industries, use assessment centres as final deciders. For example, IBM receives approximately 10,000 applications a year for its graduate trainee positions. About 2,500 to 3,000 will be invited to regional days for a first interview and tests; of those 50–60 per cent will be invited to an assessment centre. At the centres, candidates are assigned for the 24-hour assessment period to experienced IBM managers and recent trainees.

An assessment centre day

This starts with tea, biscuits and reassurance.

Exercise 1 (last 45 minutes)

Analysing information and drawing conclusions in writing. You are advised to use a calculator.

Exercise 2

Group assessment involving teamwork and planning. Assessors look for individual contributions and evidence of practical thinking.

Exercise 3

45 minutes presentation about IBM with questions. You are advised to listen carefully since using this information wisely at a later stage indicates keenness.

Lunch

You are not assessed on your etiquette or conversational abilities or so they say!

Exercise 4

Candidates are given a topic to prepare for a presentation on day two.

Exercise 5

Further exercises to test team-working skills and problem-solving abilities followed by a 4-person group 'situational' interview, testing verbal reasoning skills.

Exercise 6

In pairs, candidates are given a business-related issue where they have to agree an approach. They then use negotiating and influencing skills in discussion with other pairs.

Finally

The day ends with traditional interview with a single assessor. Why do you want the job? Do you have any questions?

Final decisions are made by the assessors working together, each with an equal say.

The ADVICE – TRY TO RELAX. It always sounds easier to say than to do.

Figure 4.20 *An assessment centre day (Source: The Guardian 19 July 1999)*

Testing for other skills and abilities

Businesses use many other tests for applicants, such as:

- logical reasoning tests – these measure a person's ability to solve problems by thinking logically on the basis of the information provided

- numerical reasoning tests – these measure a person's ability to work competently with numbers and solve problems based on data in various forms such as diagrams, graphs and statistics
- verbal reasoning tests – these measure a person's ability to use language and the written word; it usually means doing tasks such as reading and writing letters, reports and instructions
- technical tests – these aim to test candidates in the following ways:
  - the ability to understand technical ideas expressed in mathematical form
  - the ability to interpret shapes and patterns (diagram reasoning)
  - the ability to understand how things work (mechanical reasoning)
- clerical tests – these aim to test clerical skills; most secretarial agencies screen employees for speed of data input and accuracy
- observation tests – these aim to measure a candidate's powers of observation. Prospective police officers, for example, may be shown a series of video clips of a car break-in. They are then asked questions about the car registration, colour of the vehicle, type of vehicle, a description of the person, etc.

Want to know more?

Getting to grips with graphology

An alternative to psychometric tests, graphology is the analysis of handwriting to uncover intelligence, behaviour patterns, etc. It is widely used in France. How hard you press when you write, the size of your writing, the spaces between words and the slant and style of letters are all examined.

CASE STUDY

Inner values

Many occupational psychologists have their own tests for assessing applicants. For example, Criterion Partnership requires candidates to select, rank and then discuss value statements such as 'money and status', 'opportunity to make independent decisions' and 'I need approval at work'. Candidates are also asked to discuss what they believe have been the causes of positive or negative work experiences. Candidates who blame themselves for negative events may be considered not to have the emotional stamina to deal with everyday business problems such as customer complaints.

CVs and application forms

There is no right or wrong way of putting together a CV. Virtually everyone has different ideas about the best way to do it. But most employers, careers teachers and advisers agree that it should be

- simple
- clear
- short – two pages maximum
- positive.

It usually includes:

1. personal details: name, address, telephone number, date of birth, age and nationality
2. education – dates, names and addresses of schools, colleges, universities attended and details of the qualifications obtained
3. employment – dates, employers' names and addresses, job title, main responsibilities and achievements for each job held
4. interests – hobbies, sports and leisure activities
5. other information – details of key skills which would demonstrate your suitability for the position
6. references – name, addresses and job title of:
   i) employer
   ii) someone who has known the candidate for some time and can provide a character reference.

Table 4.5 Designing a CV

DO	DON'T
• Highlight key skills and achievements	• Use jargon
• Write a CV to suit the job being applied for	• Use complicated language – plain English is best
• Know your CV inside out so that you can talk about it confidently at an interview	• Copy someone else's
• Word process it – check for typing errors and spelling mistakes	• Make it up!
• Update it all the time	• Use photocopies which are dirty and crooked
	• Use scraps of paper or scruffy envelopes

Figure 4.21

The following CV is for a college or school leaver.

Name:	Jane Ann Ahmed
Address:	74 North Rd
	Canterbury CT17 1AJ
Telephone:	01227 910784
Date of Birth:	19th October 1983
Nationality:	British
Marital Status:	Single

Education

1994–1999	Frensham School for Girls
	25 Deal Road
	Canterbury
	Kent CT17 8BY
GCSEs:	English C, Maths A*, French D, Chemistry C, Physics C
1999–2001	Canterbury College
	Dover Road
	Canterbury
	Kent CT1 3AJ

GNVQ Advanced in Business. Distinction
NVQ 2 Business Administration
RSA CLAIT

Employment

1999–2001	Sainsbury's Homebase, Canterbury – Cashier
2000	Barclays Bank plc, Canterbury – Customer Service work experience – 6 weeks

Voluntary Work

Since Year 11 at school, I have worked at the local Old People's home, running shopping errands. I find this work rewarding and stimulating and would like to continue with this if I can.

Other Skills

I can use a word processor (Word) as well as databases (Access) and spreadsheets (Excel). I am also learning to drive.

Interests

I played netball for the school team. I am the Captain of the College netball team. I also like embroidery and have recently started a diving course at the local swimming baths.

Additional Information

I am a good team player and get on well with people. I am very focused on the task in hand. Since joining Canterbury College I have joined the Leisure Club and the Drama Group. I have appeared in a number of plays at the college.

References

Rees Jones	Karen McCafferty
Personnel Manager	Course Tutor
Sainsbury's/Homebase	Canterbury College
Canterbury	Dover Road
	Canterbury CT1 3AJ
	01227 811188

Figure 4.22 *Curriculum vitae*

Some businesses specifically ask you not to send a CV but to fill in an application form instead. It contains more or less the same information but it means it is more readily compared with other applicants since they are all in the same format. You must do as they ask.

APPLICATION FORM
PRIVATE AND CONFIDENTIAL

Applications are invited from women and men from all sections of the community who have the necessary attributes to carry out the job, irrespective of marital status, disability, race, colour, nationality, ethnicity, national origin or religion.

Post applied for   Nursery Nurse
Full name   Jade McKenny
Address   19 Dover Road
Sandwich
Kent
Postcode   CT25 10Z
Tel. no.   01304 791791
Date of birth   30.09.82
Do you have a full driving licence?   Yes

EDUCATION

School/College	Qualifications Achieved	Grade	Date
Sandwich Technology School	GCSE Maths	C	1998
	English	C	1998
	History	B	1998
	Geography	C	1998
	Sociology	B	1998
Thanet College, Broadstairs	BTEC GNVQ in Health and Social Care	Merit	2000
	First Aid Certificate	Pass	1999
	Food Hygiene Certificate	Pass	1999

Please give details and dates of relevant courses you have attended

July 1999	Pitman Training Canterbury	Word (Proficiency level): Distinction
July 2000	Pitman Training Canterbury	Excel (Proficiency level): Distinction

WORK HISTORY

Employer's Name and Address	From	To	Brief details of duties	Reason for leaving
Tibbitots Day Nursery 17 Brighton Rd Deal CT79 4JB	September 2000	present	Nursery assistant in baby unit	I would like promotion

FURTHER INFORMATION *(continue on another sheet if necessary)*
Please write about why you are applying for this post. You are also encouraged to write about anything else you wish to have taken into account which supports your application, and mention your hobbies, spare time activities, interests, membership of voluntary organisations, etc.

At Tibbitots Nursery I work in the baby unit with children under 6 months old. I would now like to widen my experience so that I can take on more responsibility and progress to group/room leader.

I enjoy taking part in the extracurricular activities like the summer and Christmas fairs, the Nativity Play, the Christmas Party and the Harvest Festival. I am a polite and co-operative person and like to apply myself to the task in hand.

I belong to the Sailing Club in Sandwich and regularly visit the gym to keep fit. Since I left school I have continued to help an elderly neighbour, taking her dog for a walk every evening and fetching shopping/running errands. I find this very rewarding and intend to continue as long as I can.

REFERENCES
Please give names, addresses and telephone numbers of two referees, one of whom should be your present or most recent employer.
References will be taken up after the interview.

1	**Name**	Keith Brown	2	**Name**	Jane Tierney
	Address	Tibbitots Day Nursery 17 Brighton Rd Deal CT79 4BJ		**Address**	Thanet College Ramsgate Road Broadstairs Kent CT11 4ZQ
	Occupation	Manager		**Occupation**	Child care tutor
	Tel. no.	01304 711111		**Tel. no.**	01843 605049

How did you learn about this post? Advertisement in the Kent Messenger

DECLARATION

1 I acknowledge that an appointment, if offered, will be subject to satisfactory medical clearance. Currently, I am in good health.

2 I declare that I have not been convicted of any criminal offence, spent or otherwise. This post is exempt from the provisions of the Rehabilitation of Offenders Act.

3 I declare that the information given on this form is correct and understand that on appointment any misleading statements or deliberate omissions will be regarded as grounds for disciplinary action.

Signature *J. McKenny*   **Date**   13 August 00

FOR PERSONNEL/SHORTLISTING PANEL ONLY
Shortlist/decline with reason
Date of interview _____
Panel members _____
Decision with reason _____

Figure 4.23 Application form

Six tips for effective letters of application

- **Demonstrate your qualities by examples of experience and achievements rather than unsupported statements and vague generalisations.**

- **Don't bore the reader with every last detail of your achievements. Aim for a maximum of six to eight main points and a page and a half of text.**

- **Make life easier for the selectors. Your opening paragraph needs to engage their attention and make them want to continue reading. Attributes they are looking for should be clearly illustrated.**

- **Put your draft letter aside for a day and then review it. Invariably you will find things that you can express more persuasively.**

- **Get somebody else to proofread your final draft. We all have our presentational blind spots.**

- **Don't include anything that you will not be able to demonstrate or justify at interview, and remember to keep a copy for pre-interview revision.**

Source: *Times Educational Supplement* **17 July 1998**

Other relevant information

If you are applying for a job you will want to send a letter or provide additional information with your application. This should show clearly and concisely that you match the selector's requirements and should emphasise your abilities, skills and experience. The easiest way to do this is to work from the job description.

Eight easy steps

- List the main requirements of the job.
- List the most important qualities needed.
- Think about any attributes or qualities that are important but not mentioned in the job description.
- For each of the areas listed give examples of activities and achievements which show your strengths.
- If you are using a CV, present the letter in standard business layout.
- Do not be too formal – keep it light and try to let your personality show through.
- Find out whom to address the letter to – try not to use Sir or Madam as it is very impersonal.
- Re-read the letter and cut it down to a minimum. Keep sentences short. Sound enthusiastic and full of energy.

A CTIVITY

You didn't get the job ... Ouch!

Using e-mail has its downside. Researchers at New York University say people are better at conveying bad news via computer than on the phone or face to face. Try it out for yourselves. Divide yourselves into groups.

1 Get a copy of the local paper, select a job that you can all apply for and write your CV and a letter of application.

2 Using the guidance below, draw up a critical appraisal of the CV of someone else in the group. Subdivide the group into three equal units. One group should do their appraisals (individually) using e-mail, one group should write their appraisal by hand and the third has to deliver their verdicts face to face.

3 Review all of the appraisals.

4 Which group was the most openly critical?

Seeing through the CV and application form

Companies look through these very carefully. They are concerned with:

- *Layout*: Is it tidy and accurate (which suggests attention to detail and an organised person) or crammed and untidy (which might suggest a chaotic mind)?

- *Language*: Is the CV full of bland words which show no real personality or originality of thought? Weak words include challenge, liaised, involved, whereas strong words include led, handled and managed.
- *Dates*: Are there any gaps? 1999–2000 could mean 1 December 1999 to 31 January 2000, i.e. two months, not a whole year.
- *Achievements*: Does the candidate describe the role they've had or the result? What should it be? Look at the title 'ACHIEVEMENTS'. Do the achievements match the criteria laid down in the Person Specification?
- *Inconsistencies*: Does the title of the job match the description of what the person has done? Why not? Are there reasons for that, such as the job changing faster than the job description?
- *Interests*: Most CVs and application forms ask candidates to list their hobbies and interests outside work. What do they say about the candidate's personality? They should not be taken at face value. There is a world of difference between being a member and an *active* member. The former has a membership card and sits at home whereas the latter has get up and go.

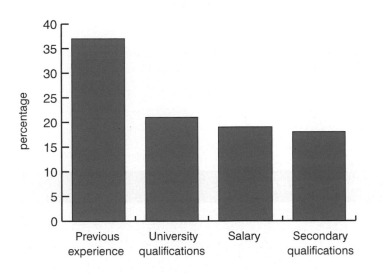

Figure 4.24 *The big porkies: what employers say are the most common lies on CVs*
Source: The Guardian *15 January 2000*

Recruitment costs money

Recently unemployment has been falling and skills shortages are beginning to appear. This is prompting workers to switch jobs. According to recent research, staff turnover in 1999 in almost every industry had increased. One in three craft and manual skilled workers had changed jobs.

Employers are now spending more to replace departing employees. It costs between £3,600 and £4,600 to replace one employee and for managers this increases to £5,000. Recruitment is costly but it is even more expensive if the organisation recruits the wrong person!

So why does recruitment cost so much?

Recruiting

The actual cost of filling the post includes the time taken to analyse what the job entails, writing the job description and advertising in the press, job centres, etc. Then there is the expense of interviewing and selection itself, including space usage, test analysis and feedback, telephone calls, photocopying, stamps, assessor's time, selection panel's time, etc. Firms may also have the cost of house removal and travel expenses for the successful candidate and one mustn't forget the additional costs of using specialist agencies or headhunters.

Training

This is the cost of bringing the new employee up to speed both through formal training and support from existing employees.

Productivity

As departing employees prepare to leave, their productivity (output) tends to decline. Similarly since new recruits are learning the job, their productivity may be lower.

Net savings
Internet based recruitment agencies maintain a database of job hunters.

What does it cost?

- **Job hunters usually pay nothing. They complete a CV or application form online.**

- **Companies looking for employees search the recruitment agencies' databases.**

- **Employers draw up a list of people they are interested in and pay a fee to release the CVs.**

- **If the prospective employers want to interview anyone they have to pay an additional fee to get the candidate's address, telephone number, etc.**

Want to know more?

If you are applying for jobs online, there are four key things to remember.

- Do not attach a CV to the application form – paste it into the main body of the text. Potential employers may ignore an attachment as they are concerned about viruses and their software may not be able to read it.
- Include the reference number for the specific job. This makes subsequent searches of any database more likely to select your application.
- Use words that are likely to be identified by a search for relevant experience, e.g. job titles and qualifications.
- Use the latest buzzwords, e.g. e-commerce, online, etc. This helps your application to be selected by the industry-standard search software.

It's not just the cost

Besides affecting an organisation's 'bottom line' or profits, hiring also affects the following factors.

Morale

If the new employee doesn't fit into the existing team the enthusiasm of the new recruit will quickly wane, as will that of the existing employees.

Culture

If a company hires a maverick or wild-card recruit when it needed a corporate clone, the culture of the organisation can quickly be affected, sometimes for the better, but most teams would argue that it is for the worse.

Reputation

If a company makes a lot of mistakes in hiring, it may quickly become known as an unreliable, hire and fire firm. This affects its ability to recruit successfully in the future as most employees are looking for some stability at work.

Effective interviewing

Modern thinking views successful interviewing as a two-way appraisal of a possible mutual business opportunity. Employers know the candidate can input data and use spreadsheets effectively, but what else does the candidate have to offer? Companies therefore look to see what other core competences are on offer and ask questions in such a way that they can find them.

> **Key term**
>
> **Core competences** – the ability to perform activities that are central to a particular job or occupation. It also includes the ability to transfer skills and knowledge to new situations and problems. And it includes qualities such as personal effectiveness and working with others in the workplace.

ⓒASE STUDIES

Are you behaviourally challenged?

After finding out that 80 per cent of its disciplinary cases arose from behaviour issues, the California Health & Welfare Agency changed its recruitment processes to concentrate on behavioural competences such as emotional IQ and stability.

Up and away

The three areas of competency most commonly listed for obtaining professional status pay in the US are:

- technical knowledge (91%)
- problem solving (77%)
- teamwork (76%)

The NHS – Are you competent?

Ealing NHS Trust introduced a pilot competency-based assessment programme for nurses.

- It was based on the idea of 'clinical ladders' so that nurses could progress according to their level of competence as housekeeper, healthcare worker, general nurse and nurse clinician.
- Each area has different competency levels, i.e. competent, intermediate and proficient.

Results are promising – lower nurse dropout rates and reduced sickness rates.

A CTIVITY

So you think you can get the job?

You may think you've got all the right qualities for the job but can you answer the REAL TOUGHIES?

1 Why do you want to work here?
2 Describe for us your ethics.
3 Why are manhole covers round?
4 Tell me how you handled a confrontation with a co-worker.
5 What went wrong in your last job?
6 Describe a situation in which your work was criticised.
7 Tell us about the last time you lost your temper.
8 If you were the boss, what would you change about this company?

Source: '101 Toughest Interview Questions', Daniel Porot and Frances Bolles Haynes

Want to know more?

www.Job-interview.net

Difficult questions often arise in the following areas.

Approach to work

Organisations need to find out how the candidate works. Bureaucrats are not very flexible and concentrate on the procedures, whereas smart workers focus on the results. Questions you may be asked include:

- What do you find is the best way to get things done for a project set by your tutor?
- How do you manage your time if the deadline is in six weeks time?

Perseverance

Organisations need to know whether candidates will fail when they meet their first difficulty. Questions you may be asked include:
- What has been the most challenging project you've done so far?
- What difficulties did you experience?
- How did you overcome them?

Achievement

Employers want to know how successful candidates have been in the past and what value has been added to your previous employer's business. Questions you may be asked include:
- Can you tell us about a project you've led or been involved with in the last year which had a significant impact on your organisation?
- What sort of impact did it have on (say) sales?

Values

Companies usually try to fit the person to the job, bearing in mind the organisation's culture. However, some companies look for the candidates with different skills if they're trying to change the way things are done. Questions you may be asked include:
- If you were looking back over your career to date, how would you assess it?
- What criteria would you use?

Motivation

Employers want to know what motivates the candidate. Is it money, status, working in a team or alone? Questions you may be asked include:
- Why are you interested in this post?

Weaknesses

These are as important as learning experiences and employers will want to explore any failures. They will want to know whether the candidate used them positively, constructively and learnt from them. Questions you may be asked include:
- Tell us about your largest failure. How did you deal with it?

Social skills/interpersonal skills

Organisations need people who can work in teams and lead them. They are on the lookout for people with a quick temper or a puffed-up opinion of themselves because people management would then be more difficult. Organisations are looking for people who can get on with most people. That doesn't mean everyone or preclude arguments, but someone who gets on with no one would be a disaster. Questions you may be asked include:

- The marketing department is very touchy about deadlines for copy. How would you handle them?
- What would you do if they reported your team to the manager?

Initiative

Employers need to know whether the candidate needs a lot of support or can they work on their own without needing to be told? It is particularly important to establish this for management or supervisory positions. Questions you may be asked include:

- What have you done with your team that was your own idea?
- How did you plan it?
- What were the outcomes?

Balance

Increasingly companies are looking for 'balanced' individuals. They are not keen to employ people who are 'all work and no play' or 'all play and no work'. Questions you may be asked include:

- What hobbies do you have?
- Why do you enjoy them?

Want to know more?

For many candidates, one of the hardest questions is: 'Don't you think you're over-qualified for this job?' Possible answers include:

- When I consider the skills I have assembled, I consider myself a good match for this job.
- I feel I have many positive things I can offer to the organisation.
- I think character and relevant experience are just as important as qualifications.
- I am confident that I can perform the tasks required to a very high standard.

CASE STUDY

Netscape recruitment

Netscape frequently employs 'hackers'. It recently had three students it offered jobs to who were able to identify errors in its software systems.

Why? Netscape recognises that it can learn from individuals who can break into its systems.

CASE STUDY

The Microsoft process

A senior manager is always involved in the process of interviewing. If Microsoft is not interested in who it takes on, neither will anyone else be.

Little emphasis is put on written tests. Recruits may be able to produce perfect test answers but these tests do not identify those who can think creatively. One way of doing this is through the use of brainteasers such as 'How much water flows through the Thames?' Microsoft is not looking for the right answer but how you would go about solving the problem. Does the candidate ask the right questions such as: 'How long is the Thames? What is the flow rate at pertinent points along the river?'

Interview pitfalls – Does the interviewer always get it right?

Interviewing alone

It is better to use several people in the process rather than to use one person's judgement, which may be flawed. Most organisations use a panel with individual members looking at the job role and candidates from different perspectives.

Talking too much

The idea of an interview is to find out as much as possible about the candidate. If the interviewer does all the talking how will he or she learn anything about the candidate?

Gut reaction

Many interviewers use this method of selection but it isn't as successful as exploring the strengths and weaknesses of the individual.

Winging it

Many interviewers simply do not prepare adequately beforehand. They read the CV/job description two minutes before and really don't have an understanding of who they are looking at before diving in. They frequently end up with unsuitably qualified recruits whom they have to get rid of or who leave very quickly because the job isn't the right one for them.

Closed minds

Interviewers frequently have a clear view of what they want and don't budge from it. It may be that something they haven't considered as a plus – or a minus – makes the difference between a good appointment and a poor one.

Missing the signals

Some organisations have such a rigid interview procedure that they don't notice throwaway lines and don't follow up on important indicators. For example, an organisation looking for a legal executive may have missed the fact that the candidate was dismissed from their position for misconduct. You can be sure that the candidate won't put it on their CV. They will probably not include referees who would identify this. Similarly, references may look good but further probing may establish that the candidate has had a long-term sickness problem with their existing employer. The present employer may well write a good reference to get rid of them! It is therefore essential to question candidates' backgrounds, experience and personality very carefully.

Not allowing the candidate to quiz you

Interviews may be so candidate-centred that the interviewee doesn't have the opportunity to question the interviewer. The sort of questions the candidate asks frequently shows the kind of things they're looking for in a job.

Halo effect

Some interviewers have their own prejudices and allow one feature of the interviewee to override all other factors in a favourable or unfavourable way.

So you've had the interview. What next?

If you get an interview but don't get the job, it is a good idea to review your performance to give yourself an idea of the things you need to improve upon (see Table 4.7).

Table 4.6 Appearing smart

DO	DON'T
<ul><li>Prepare thoroughly</li><li>Identify key skills and research the organisation</li><li>Think about consulting an interview coach</li><li>Look the interviewer in the eye but don't stare</li><li>Be prepared for 'what if' questions</li></ul>	<ul><li>Undersell yourself. You don't need to go over the top but if you don't say what you can do no one else will</li><li>Appear over-interested in salary, holidays or company car. The right time to start bargaining is when you are offered the job</li></ul>

Brian Krueger reckons that good vocabulary and enunciation are critical success factors. If you have 'lazy lips' practise saying your words more clearly. Use a mirror. Remember James Dean you are not!

Table 4.7 *Analysing your performance*

How Did You Do?	Yes	No	Notes
1 Were you on time?			
2 Did you have time to go to the toilet, comb your hair, look through any notes you've made?			
3 Would you change anything next time? If so, what?			
4 Did you find the tests difficult? Why?			
5 What do you need to practise or brush up on next time?			
6 What did you wear when you went into the interview? Did you feel comfortable and confident in what you wore? What would you do differently next time?			
7 What did you forget?			
8 Did you feel comfortable with the process? Why not?			
9 Did you get on well with the panel of interviewers? Why not?			
10 Could you have avoided this? How?			
11 What questions did you find difficult to answer? Why? How could you improve your replies?			
12 Did you say something awful? What was it? How could you stop yourself doing this in the future?			
13 Did you ask any questions? Were they appropriate? If not, why?			
14 How did you leave the room?			
15 Did you forget to say something crucial? What?			
16 Did the interview go well, OK or badly? Why? What could you do to improve your performance?			

NOW THINK AGAIN

Were you really there? Were you listening actively to the questions and answering them in the best possible way? Do you need to pitch your application differently? It is worth visiting your Careers Service/Advisor again and finding out where your talents are and where you need to direct them.

TALK TO SOMEONE NOW

Contracts of employment

To remain competitive, businesses need to develop new products and services, and identify new markets. This requires careful people management. There isn't one way to meet the staffing needs of a business. Each business is different and requires its own staffing solution.

CASE STUDY

Official statistics show that 70 per cent of new jobs created between 1995 and 1998 have not been permanent full-time ones. Between 1992 and 1996 the number of temporary workers rose by 30 per cent, with fixed-term contracts and agency temping increasing by similar amounts. An Institute of Employment Studies survey found that more than half the firms in its sample were employing temporary staff while a further 17 per cent had done so in the past.

CASE STUDY

Tesco's core hours

Figure 4.25 *Meeting the workers' needs*

Tesco has flexible working arrangements which:
- aim to improve customer service while containing or reducing employment
- use the concept of 'core hours'. Workers are employed for 10–16 fixed 'core' hours a week and additional flexible hours, when required, up to a maximum of 31 hours.

Employees joining the scheme enjoy the same employment benefits, e.g. holidays and sick pay, as other employees. Michelle Wilder, a checkout operator, says: 'I work at Tesco's on a flexible contract. It suits me because I don't always want to work a full week but now the children are grown up I can work longer hours when they need me to – the extra money is always useful! Some of my friends work in shops with zero hours contracts which means they are never really sure when or if they will be working. They find it difficult to plan around work because they always have the feeling that if they say no they may not be asked again.'

Zero hours contracts,
page 19

CASE STUDY

What happened to job security?

Figure 4.26 Using peripheral workers creates more flexible working

'During the late eighties Lloyds, like all banks, was looking at making major job cuts. I was managing the settlements department and with the introduction of new computerised systems for collections and payments junior and middle management roles were to be cut. I was sure I wouldn't be one of those but when I got my brown envelope making me redundant I was devastated. So much for a secure job in a bank! I was unemployed for six months which felt like forever. It is really hard when you think you might be on the scrapheap at 33. I was pretty hard to live with and I sometimes wonder whether that was one of the reasons that a couple of years later my wife Jill had to take early retirement with stress. In the end I got this job with Barclays Bank inputting data on a computer at home. At the start I expected it to be a temporary job until the prospects in banking improved again but now it looks as though it's permanent. My wife suffers ill health so it makes things easier working at home although I still go in to the office one day a week. It's also becoming more interesting. At first I was just given a computer and a modem and spent all day working on that. Now I also spend part of each day speaking to customers. The pay is a lot lower but I don't have the costs of going to work or dressing smartly.'

Another approach taken by businesses is to have a core of full-time workers who perform key tasks. Everything else is done by groups of peripheral workers. This creates more flexible working and includes staff who are:

Key terms

Key terms

Part-time workers have permanent contracts, but work set or flexible hours. Part-time usually refers to anything below 30 hours per week.
Fixed-term workers have full- or part-time contracts but they are taken on for a particular project. When this is over they may or may not be re-engaged.
Temporary workers are usually taken on to cover peaks in demand, maternity leave, etc. They are usually paid on an hourly or weekly basis on the clear understanding that the work is of a temporary nature.
Outsourced workers – many businesses have support or peripheral functions such as cleaning, catering and IT, which are increasingly being transferred to a specialist supplier rather than provided in-house.
Teleworkers – where companies allow employees to work from home.

- part time
- fixed term
- temporary
- outsourced
- teleworkers.

The number of different contractual arrangements has grown enormously in the last ten years. Traditional contracts are still widely used but a recent Institute of Employment Studies survey shows that 'In many organisations core employees with traditional contracts are working on projects with specialists on fixed-term contracts, freelancers, self-employed consultants, employees from other organisations and company workers who work across the organisation and also outside the organisation.'

The upside of flexible contracts

Most companies argue that flexible contracts reduce business's costs. There are other benefits. For example, if a weak Information Technology department is outsourced to a major external supplier, the quality of IT will improve. Businesses are able to use the employees' flexibility to manage the peaks and troughs in demand throughout the year. These contracts can suit employees who have young families or elderly relatives or wish to pursue other interests alongside work.

The downside of flexible contracts

Many companies meet resistance to new-style contracts and sometimes the most experienced employees decide to leave and become freelance. This can create problems of confidentiality since these people can now work for competitors and they frequently do. They may not always be available to work for their original employer and organisations end up with a less flexible workforce.

The best freelancers are always in demand and are able to increase their fees. This means that a firm's costs may actually go up. As many line managers, desperate for staff, do not have the bargaining skills to deal with professional negotiators, costs can rise. Many companies find it easier just to renew contracts even though they might not have the best person for the job or it is very expensive.

The labour turnover rates in companies using flexible contracts often rise. The cost of recruitment, training and managing new staff can be quite significant. As part-time workers often get less training and lower pay, there can be an impact on the quality of the company's products.

Labour turnover rate,
page 9

CASE STUDY

Have organisations got it right?

In the early twentieth century mass production used flexible working: casual shifts, temporary work, lay offs, zero hour contracts. This led to unhappy employees who did not know when they would work. It was Henry Ford who discovered the hidden costs of flexibility and gave his employees regular contracts with higher pay. Ford said at the time: 'This is one of the finest cost-cutting moves we ever made.'

Figure 4.27 *The experience of Ford's: flexible working in 1914
The Ford Motor Co. Ltd*

The rights and responsibilities of employers and employees

A business organisation involves complicated relationships between everyone who works in it. If you buy a book there is a simple economic relationship between yourself and the person from whom you buy it. As long as you pay the agreed amount at the right time there are unlikely to be any other obligations upon you. For instance, it is unlikely to be a condition of the purchase that you actually read the book. An employment contract is much more complicated. Although there is an economic component there are also very strong social features. You give up much of your power and independence in exchange for an economic benefit: your salary or wage.

A clear definition of the rights and responsibilities of employers and employees is essential so that neither side is able to take advantage of this relationship. Without these definitions an employer might, for instance, insist upon an employee working excessive hours. Similarly, an employee might refuse to perform certain tasks that are essential to the operation for which he or she is responsible. The most important of these rights and responsibilities are contained in employment law. Some of the more important Acts of Parliament are mentioned below (see

Appendix for fuller details). Others may well be included in the contract of employment that you sign when you first agree to take on a particular job. This is discussed later on.

Employee rights

Some of the main rights of employees (and therefore responsibilities of employers) include the following.

A written agreement of the terms and conditions of employment

This contract of employment will set out the date on which the employment will start, the job title and details of pay, benefits and hours of work. All employees are entitled to a contract within one month of starting a job.

Written Statement of the Main Terms and Conditions of Employment under the Employment Protection (Consolidation) Act 1978

Relating to the Employment of Teresa Bannerman
By Trainee Company Ltd and correct at 17 August 2001

*Any alteration to the terms and conditions of your employment will, within one month of the date of any such alteration, be notified to you in writing.

Continuous Employment
Your employment with the Company began on 3 August 2001 and any employment with a previous employer does not count as part of your period of employment.

Job Title
You are employed as an Administration Assistant but will be expected to undertake other reasonable duties requested by senior staff.

Pay
You will be paid monthly by bank giro credit at the rate of £833.33 per month. It is a condition of employment that if overpayments occur, e.g. salary, sickness or holiday taken in excess of entitlement, you authorise the Company to deduct outstanding sums owed by you from your wage or terminal payment.

Hours of Work
The office is open from 7 am to 7 pm Monday to Friday. Your hours are based round the current shift system, as agreed by senior staff.

Your normal hours are 37 per week; however, the nature of the business requires flexibility and you may be required to work outside these hours if necessary. Under normal circumstances no additional payment will be made for these hours, but time off in lieu may be considered. However, where payment is made, it will be on the basis of the basic hourly rate.

All members of staff are required to attend ALL staff and planning meetings.

Holiday Entitlement
You are entitled to 21 working days per year for the first two years. This will increase annually by one day to a maximum of 25 working days. The office will close at Christmas in which case 3 days of your entitlement will need to be reserved for this purpose.

Your entitlement will be calculated pro rata to your length of service in the current holiday year which runs from 1 January to 31 December.

A minimum 2 weeks notice is required to book annual leave and 72 hours when booking individual days as holidays. Half days holiday may be considered. No more than 10 working days may be taken at any one time and only one member of staff may take annual leave at any one time; therefore early booking is advisable to avoid disappointment. Preference will be given to staff with young children who wish to book leave during school holidays. Unpaid leave will only be granted in exceptional circumstances.

In addition you are entitled to 8 statutory holidays as follows: New Year's Day**, Good Friday and Easter Monday, May Day, Spring Bank Holiday Monday, August Bank Holiday Monday, Christmas Day**, Boxing Day**. **In the event of these falling on a Saturday or Sunday, the recognised Public Holiday will be observed.

Unauthorised absence on the last working day prior to, or the first working day after, a Statutory Holiday will result in non-payment of Statutory Holiday.

Outstanding leave not taken by 31 December can only be carried over to the following year in exceptional circumstances.

Absence Due to Sickness or Injury

The following procedure must be followed if you are unable to come to work: On the first day of absence, employees must telephone the management at least two hours minimum before the start of the shift to notify the reason for absence and if possible the likely date of return. Thereafter, every reasonable effort must be made to keep the management informed of progress in order to assist with staff scheduling. You must contact the office by 4 pm the day before your return to work. If you do not ring you will be presumed absent and you position will be covered. A company self-certification form must be completed for periods of absence of up to 7 days. Thereafter, a Doctor's statement (MED3) will be needed for absence lasting 8 or more calendar days. You should continue to submit certificates until you are fit to return to work.

Failure to comply with the above procedure could affect your entitlement to benefit and render you liable to disciplinary action.

Pay Arrangements

Statutory Sick Pay will be paid in accordance with DSS requirements. No payment will be made for the first 3 waiting days in a period of incapacity for work.

Pension Scheme

The Company operates a pension scheme and no contracting-out certificate is in force for the employment in respect of which this written statement is being issued.

Notice of Termination of Employment

Notice should be given in writing in accordance with the following:

Length of Service	Employer to Employee	Employee to Employer
Up to 12 weeks	1 week	1 week
12 weeks or more	1 month	1 month

In the interests of continuity and good quality customer service more than one month's notice may be necessary. If you hold a senior position more than one month's notice will be expected. Any employee leaving without giving due notice will lose their entitlement to accrued holiday pay.

Grievance Procedure

It is important for the company and all employees that any grievance is brought to light and dealt with as quickly as possible. If you have a grievance which cannot be dealt with on an informal basis you should raise it formally, either verbally or in writing, with your supervisor or manager. Further details are set out in the Company Handbook.

Company Rules
The Company Handbook lays down rules which employees are expected to observe in order to ensure that reasonable standards of behaviour are maintained.

Disciplinary Procedure
If the management considers that the company rules are not being followed or any employee is otherwise failing to fulfil his/her requirements in a satisfactory manner, then action may be taken under the company's disciplinary procedure. Details of this are set out in the Company Handbook.

Copies of the Company Handbook are available for reference in the office.

Issued by: Trainee Company Ltd _____ (Manager)

Received by: _____ (Employee)

Date: _____

Figure 4.28 Contract of employment

Trade unions
Although anyone is legally entitled to join a union appropriate to their job, the benefits and support this can bring have decreased in many industries over the past 15 years. Legislation in the 1980s and 1990s limited trade unions' power to take industrial action and made it easier for people to be employed without belonging to a union. In addition, an increasing number of companies have derecognised unions. Whilst this enables companies to be more flexible in the way they employ and pay people, it prevents employees from having access to a large, national body that may protect their interests.

Equal pay
The Equal Pay Act 1970 and the Equal Value Amendment of 1983 ensure that men and women who do the same jobs or jobs of equal value are entitled to equal pay. This legislation was brought in to address the fact that women were paid less than men for doing exactly the same job.

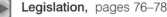 **Legislation,** pages 76–78

Discrimination at work
The Sex Discrimination Act 1975, the Race Relations Act 1976 and the Disability Discrimination Act 1995 have made it illegal to discriminate against someone on the grounds of sex, marital status, race or disability.

There is increasing pressure to ensure that people are not discriminated against because of age. In 1997 Linda Perham MP introduced a private member's bill to end age discrimination in job advertisements. The Government refused to grant it parliamentary time and the bill failed. Following consultation a voluntary code of practice has now been issued. Companies adopting the code will have formal policies to outlaw discrimination.

Figure 4.29 *'What a drag it is getting old' sang Mick Jagger, but increasing numbers of older people are bringing changes in attitudes to older workers*

Want to know more?

- The proportion of the total population over 50 has more than doubled in the last 100 years.
- By 2010 40 per cent of the labour force will be 45 or over while 16–17 year olds will make up only 17 per cent.
- In recent years there has been a dramatic fall in the proportion of economically active men aged 55 and over.

Table 4.8 Mixed age colleagues

Advantages of Mixed Age Workforce	Disadvantages of Mixed Age Workforce
Flexible multi skilled workforce	Resistant to change
Greater experience	Less fit
Higher motivation	
Increased productivity	
Reduced absence	
Wider choice of people for recruitment	

One survey shows that only 7 per cent of employers have a policy on age.

Reproduced by permission of PFD, on behalf of Ros Asquith

CASE STUDY

Experience matters

When B&Q opened their new Macclesfield store 10 years ago they decided to recruit exclusively from the over 60s. Researchers from Warwick University compared the performance of the store with others in terms of sales, profitability, staff turnover, absenteeism and overall customer satisfaction – the Macclesfield store was performing better. As a result B&Q has adopted positive policies towards older people as they believe, 'Attitude is more important than age.'

Unfair dismissal

The Employment Protection (Consolidation) Act 1978 ensures that every employee who has been with an employer for two years or more cannot be unfairly dismissed. In general the reasons that may be thought a fair cause for dismissal include inability to do the job, misconduct, the company no longer being able to employ the person (for instance where changes in regulations occur) and where the company no longer requires that particular job to be done. In this last case the job is termed redundant and it is not permissible to employ anyone to replace the person whose job has been made redundant. If employees feel that they have been unfairly dismissed they can take their case to an employment tribunal.

Safe working conditions

The Health and Safety at Work Act 1974 requires every employer to have a written policy on health and safety, to make employees aware of their responsibilities and to train them to do their jobs in a healthy and safe fashion and to ensure that working conditions are healthy and safe.

Training and professional development

In most cases the only training which employers are legally responsible for providing is health and safety training. Even so, many employers recognise that they have a responsibility to provide employees with sufficient training to do their jobs properly. In addition, some companies have policies that state what opportunities for development should be made available to employees. For instance, a company may have a policy to promote people internally wherever possible.

A summary of employee rights is shown in Table 4.9.

Employer rights

Employees have certain responsibilities (and therefore employers can expect these things from their employees). There is a distinction between explicit terms and conditions which are written into the

Table 4.9 *Employee rights summarised*

Employee rights	Length of service necessary
Statement of terms and conditions	One month
Minimum period of notice	One month
Not to be unfairly dismissed	One year
Not to be dismissed due to pregnancy	Immediate
Written reasons for dismissal	Two years
Not to be discriminated against on the grounds of race, sex or disability	Immediate
Not to be discriminated against on the grounds of health and safety complaints	Immediate
Not to be dismissed on the grounds of claiming statutory rights	Immediate
Time off for ante-natal care	Immediate
Maternity pay	Six months
Maternity leave	Immediate
Right to additional maternity leave	One year
Guarantee payments	One month
Itemised pay statements	Immediate
Redundancy payments	Two years
Pay during suspension on medical grounds	One month
Back pay and holiday pay if employer insolvent	Immediate
Time off to look for work and/or arrange training in case of redundancy	Two years
Time off for public duties, e.g. local councillor	Immediate
Time off for duties as recognised independent trade union officer	Immediate
Time off to carry out duties as a safety representative	Immediate
Deduction from wages	Immediate

employment contract and implicit obligations which are sometimes called the 'psychological contract' between employer and employee. These are what you feel you ought to do although it is not specifically stated. Responsibilities may include the following.

Being available, willing and able to work

This includes a good record of attendance and punctuality. It also entails having, or obtaining, the right qualifications and skills. It may, for instance, be a condition of someone's employment as an accountant that they attend at least 20 hours of professional development training a year. Likewise, if a salesperson's job requires a clean driving licence, if they lose their licence their employer may be entitled to dismiss them.

Taking reasonable care and skill

If an employee continues to do the job to a low standard despite reasonable training and support, an employer may be able to dismiss him or her for incompetence. In addition, employees have a duty under the Health and Safety at Work Act 1974 to take reasonable care for the safety of themselves and others.

Taking proper care of property

Equipment and other physical resources can cost an organisation a great deal of money. Whilst it is the employer's responsibility to ensure that employees are properly trained to use the equipment, employees must use the equipment in such a way as to prevent avoidable damage.

Following any reasonable instructions given

It is assumed that people who are more senior within an organisation, or who have special responsibilities for particular areas (e.g. for Health and Safety), have a better understanding of what needs to be done to meet the organisation's objectives. For this reason, many contracts of employment designate a line manager who has the authority to instruct the employee in his or her job. Reasonable instructions do not include requiring anyone to do anything that might be illegal or anything that is completely out of the normal course of one's work (for instance requiring an accounts clerk to serve in the canteen) or for which you have not had reasonable training.

Acting in good faith

There is an assumption that employees will always act with the best of intentions and in a responsible fashion. This recognises that people do make errors and this is acceptable but if someone intentionally does or says something harmful to the employer this may be a breach of contract.

How the law is changing

Employment law is constantly changing owing to the nature of work and technology. Employers need to review their policies and procedures regularly to make sure they comply with the law. In 1998 over 10,000 actions were brought before Industrial Tribunals by employees.

An unfair dismissal verdict may cost an employer more than £50,000 in addition to the costs of bad publicity and the effect on other employees. Compensation awards made in sex, race and disability discrimination cases include an award of £358,259 to a computer operator who suffered racial abuse and was unfairly dismissed from a London borough council; and an award of over £230,000 to a former employee of another council who suffered sexual discrimination when she was given her notice.

The major changes

The Employment Relations Act came into force at the end of 1999. Its main features include the following:

- an upper limit for unfair dismissal of £50,000
- employees with fixed-term contracts of one year or more cannot waive their unfair dismissal rights
- right of individual workers to be accompanied by a work colleague or trade union official at serious disciplinary or grievance hearings
- right to reasonable unpaid time off during working hours to deal with domestic emergencies
- increase in maternity leave to a minimum of 18 weeks and a reduction of the qualifying period from two years to one year
- right to at least three months unpaid parental leave for childbirth or adoption covering the period from birth to five years
- right to trade union recognition in companies with more than 20 employees, where a majority of employees voting in a ballot decide in favour. This must add up to at least 40 per cent of the workforce.

Unfair dismissal

The Unfair Dismissal and Statement of Reasons for Dismissal (Variation of Qualifying Period) Order 1999 protects employees from unfair dismissal if they have been employed for at least one year. There are some exceptions to this where the protection applies immediately, e.g. when dismissal is for trade union activity, pregnancy, health and safety reasons or for asserting a statutory right.

Minimum wage

The National Minimum Wage Act 1998 and National Minimum Wage Regulations 1999 cover those with a contract of employment plus a wider group who undertake work classed as agency or temporary work. The minimum wage was introduced at £3.60 per hour with £3.00 per hour for 18 to 21 year olds. These rates were raised to £3.70 and £3.20 per hour in 2000 and are expected to rise by another 40p per hour in 2001. Workers under 18 are excluded, as are apprentices under the age of 26 who are in their first year of apprenticeship.

Hours of work

The Working Time Regulations 1998 also set a working time limit of an average of 48 hours per week and apply to all workers over school leaving age with a contract of employment as well as those doing agency and temporary work. The Regulations exclude those in transport, sea fishing, other work at sea, and doctors in training. They also exclude the armed forces, the police, and the civil protection services. The Regulations also provide for the following.

Rest breaks

Adult workers are entitled to one day off each week, 11 consecutive hours rest per day and a 20-minute rest break if their working day is longer than six hours. Young workers are entitled to two days per week, 12 hours rest per day and a 30-minute rest break if they work longer than four hours.

Paid annual leave

Workers are entitled to four weeks annual leave which can include public and bank holidays. Workers also have the right to pro rata payment for holidays which they have not taken where their employment ends during the leave year.

Private information

The Data Protection Act 1998 contains rules on personnel records including access, disclosure and control over personal information held by employers. It covers computerised data and information in manual filing systems.

Employers must look at the kind of information they collect from employees in the light of this Act's provisions on 'sensitive data'. This includes racial or ethnic origin, political and religious beliefs, trade union membership and physical or mental condition, etc. Employers can only collect and store this data with the consent of the employee.

European law

The European Union Part Time Work Directive gave part-time workers equal access to contractual employment rights. Part-time and full-time workers should be treated similarly in the provision of paid holiday, sick pay, etc. The European Works Councils Directive affects communications between the workforce and management. It gives employees rights to information and consultation and affects any company with 1,000 employees or more and at least 150 employees located in two or more Member States of the European Union.

Children at work

The Children (Protection at Work) Regulations 1998 provide for the following features:

- children must be 14 years old before they can be employed
- children are prohibited from doing anything but light work
- children over 14 are limited to eight hours of work on non-school days; the limit for school days and Sundays is two hours
- a weekly limit of 35 hours (25 if the child is under 15) per week in the school holidays
- work without a rest break of at least one hour is limited to four hours or less in any day
- children must have at least two consecutive weeks without work in school holidays.

The public interest

The Public Interest Disclosure Act 1998 protects those who blow the whistle on wrongdoing at work. It aims to cover failures to comply with legal obligations, miscarriages of justice, health and safety issues, damage to the environment, and the hiding of information.

Human rights

The Human Rights Act 1998 brought the European Convention on Human Rights into UK law. In the employment field the Act covers those who are employed by the State. It provides the right to privacy and family life, and offers redress to public sector employees if they are discriminated against in the workplace.

Lifelong learning and development

Training ensures that people have the right skills, knowledge and attitude to do a job, whether it is the job they are currently doing or one they might do in the future. Ideally training should be planned to meet organisational objectives besides providing individuals with the personal development they want. For instance, providing factory operatives with computer skills may contribute to a company's objective of increasing the level of technology in its manufacturing process. At the same time, it may provide staff with personal development through increased employability or a sense of pride in a new skill and therefore increased job satisfaction.

Employees are expected to take some responsibility for their own performance. They may be required to identify their own strengths and weaknesses during a performance review or appraisal or suggest training or development which would help them to do their jobs better or increase their worth to the business. Increasingly employees are also expected to take on some of the financial responsibility for their training.

CASE STUDY

In 1998 Dixon's Store Group launched an ambitious personnel development programme with the aim of creating a more skilled workforce to meet its business objectives. The programme was geared towards developing a training culture where employees took greater responsibility for their own training. 'We wanted to change people's perceptions of training from something which was "done to them" to something they have bought into,' said Tracy Fowler, Training Manager. 'Our training programme was designed to transfer ownership of learning from the manager to the individual.'

Source: *Professional Manager*, The Institute of Management

ACTIVITY

It's off to work we go!

Think about your own education and training: what further training do you need to follow your chosen career? Have you chosen the right career path? Try to map out the courses of development you will need to complete over the next five years. Will they lead to nationally recognised qualifications? You can check these through the Qualifications and Curriculum Authority's website at www.qca.org.uk. Where are these courses available? Keep a record of this information as you may be asked these questions at a job interview.

Want to know more?

What are individual learning accounts? What are they worth? Where can you spend them? Could you use them to contribute to your own learning? Access www.learningdirect.org to find out more.

CASE STUDY

Cool Companies

Pitney Bowes is a leading multinational provider of mailing and messaging products including faxes, photocopiers, software, etc. The company has over two million customers in 120 countries. Pitney Bowes is accredited with an Investors in People standard and this shows the company's commitment to staff training and development. The company is also included in Britain's Best Employers – the guidebook to the most attractive 100 companies to work for in the UK.

Want to know more?

Access www.pitneybowes.com.uk for more information.

Most new employees receive an induction or training programme designed to introduce them to the business's working practices. This includes the health and safety requirements, and how to report accidents, as well as where to find the photocopier and the toilets. Three of the main purposes of induction are to:

- help new staff settle in to the routine of the workplace
- establish a positive attitude towards the company so that new staff want to stay
- help new staff 'hit the ground running' and be productive from day one.

Induction training

Some training for new staff will be done away from the workplace and some will be done by experienced employees. It is fairly common to have a couple of days at the beginning which is followed up a few months later. Such training usually covers:

- a brief outline of the organisation, its background, its development, the product range, the services it offers, etc
- a brief outline of the basic conditions of employment, hours of work, holidays, pension arrangements, etc
- how wages or salaries are paid, deductions from salaries, etc
- disciplinary and grievance procedures
- rules for conduct at work
- sickness rules – who to notify, when, doctor's certificates, etc
- health and safety arrangements and requirements
- training and development
- medical and first aid facilities
- social and welfare arrangements
- canteen facilities.

Most organisations have a Staff Handbook which contains all this information and the training sessions are designed to draw attention to the relevant sections and enable newcomers to ask questions.

Table 4.10 *Getting started*

Induction Procedure for New Staff	Notes and queries
Pay and conditions	
Hours	
Rate of pay	
Time sheets	
Pay arrangements	
Sickness arrangements	
Holiday entitlement	
Time off	
Grievance and disciplinary procedures	
Confidentiality	
Training opportunities	
Health and safety	
Safety	
Safety policy	
Safe working practices	
First Aid facilities	
Smoking policy	
Hygiene standards	
Others	
Policies and procedures	
Standard of behaviour	
Standard of work	
Customer care	
Private telephone calls	

Signed Member of Staff _____

Signed Manager _____ Date _____

Mentoring

When new staff join a company or existing staff change roles they are frequently allocated a mentor who acts as a critical friend and guide. This may be formal or informal depending on the organisation but can be useful in pointing out short cuts and can speed up development. Having a mentor is about developing a relationship, usually with a close colleague to give encouragement and practical advice. The relationship is complicated, and there is no point in ignoring everything the mentor says but you have to consider your own views. The relationship should be solid enough to get through some mistakes.

Coaching

This is a similar role to that of a mentor and is based on the principles used in sport. Experienced employees with a variety of skills and expertise help less experienced staff to do their jobs better. Businesses often ask their coaches to set increasingly difficult tasks for the new person, which allows them to become more experienced and skilled in the role.

Apprenticeships

In the past virtually all skilled trades such as plumbers, electricians, carpenters and hairdressers were trained through apprenticeship schemes which could last for years and involved both on and off the job training. Young people were trained by those already possessing the qualifications and the training was paid for by the employer. In return the employee was paid a relatively low wage in the knowledge that once the apprenticeship was completed their wage rates would rise dramatically. Strong links to the trades unions ensured that the numbers taken on as apprentices were limited, which helped to keep wages high. However, this link was broken in the 1980s and the number of traditional apprenticeships declined since they were regarded as 'time served', rather than training opportunities that meet the needs of individual trainees. Nowadays time served apprenticeships are rare and have been replaced by Modern Apprenticeships and National Traineeships. These provide training in over 100 occupations.

Appraisal

Most businesses operate some form of performance appraisals where each employee's contribution is evaluated by their line manager. There are two different forms of performance appraisal: formal and informal.

Informal

Managers continually review their staff during the working day, week and year. It leads to judgements about the employee's ability and value to the organisation as well as their strengths and weaknesses.

Formal

These are held in a formal setting, usually once or twice a year, using set procedures for evaluating the contribution of individual employees. Managers and supervisors assess, record and discuss performance with their staff. Such appraisal enables employees to receive feedback on their performance and identify training and development needs, and set targets for the coming year. There is usually a written record agreed between the parties.

Appraisal is carried out for several reasons:
- to identify levels of performance and to allow employees to feel that their contribution is valued
- to review performance and set future targets following feedback
- to review an employee's potential to progress up the organisation
- to offer counselling and help
- to identify training and development needs
- to help succession planning
- to develop a more participative style of management
- to review pay on the basis of performance.

Many organisations use interviews to assess an employee's performance. This should involve an honest discussion between the job holder (often referred to as the appraisee) and his or her immediate manager or supervisor (the appraiser). It helps if the employee sees the exercise as non-threatening and takes a full part. Workers need to evaluate their strengths and weaknesses critically and be willing to discuss them openly. Employees need to give positive examples of their work and identify things that haven't been successful. This is often called self-evaluation.

The supervisor usually tries to sound out the views of the team the employee works with to evaluate his or her performance. This allows the supervisor to get examples of strengths and weaknesses to support the employee's views and to help make it more objective. This is often referred to as peer evaluation.

At the end of the appraisal interview both parties usually agree an action plan which involves the setting of targets for the individual in the context of the business's strategic plan. The supervisor also recommends a pay rise or promotion if this is appropriate in addition to identifying training and development needs. Any agreed action is then carried forward to the next round of appraisal and forms the basis for the next review and whether the targets set were met, and for discussion on whether the employer met their side of the bargain! It is often forgotten in appraisals that the management may agree pay rises or promotion on the basis of performance as well as provide relevant training courses. The management's performance should also be monitored in the review and note taken of where it has failed to deliver.

One problem with appraisals is that they can be confrontational, with workers feeling defensive and suspicious and managers appearing aggressive. The upshot is that the outcome of the interview is not an increase in productivity but a decline! Most appraisal schemes have provision for the employee to appeal if he or she feels it was unfair, biased, untrue or aggressive. To prevent appeals, most businesses value appraisal training where managers and employees are helped to understand the process and the outcomes. Where the system operates effectively and in a supportive environment the effects on output can be significant. Many employees in good appraisal schemes relish the prospect.

There is not much doubt that if it is done well appraisal helps individual workers to focus on key targets, their development needs and their career plan.

360 degree appraisal
Increasingly, companies are using appraisal techniques that recognise the views of everyone who works with a manager – the staff, working colleagues and the manager's own immediate boss. This allows a fully rounded view of any employee and not just the more limited view of the line manager. For some managers, hearing the views of their staff, and other team members, can be unsettling but many businesses believe it adds to the efficiency of appraisal and is an effective technique for identifying training and development needs.

STAFF APPRAISAL FORM

Name: _____

Your next appraisal will take place on: **Date:** _____ **Time:** _____

The purpose of the appraisal is to enable you to discuss your job performance and future with your manager. It will aim to establish:

- main purpose of your job in the coming year
- agreement on your objectives and tasks
- your training needs and future prospects.

What have you accomplished over and above the minimum requirements of your job description in the last 12 months?

_____

_____

List any difficulties you have in carrying out your work. Were there any obstacles outside your control which meant you could not do your work effectively?

_____

_____

How is your:
- timekeeping? _____
- absence rate through sickness? _____
- dress code? _____

What parts of your job do you:
- do best? _____
- do less well? _____
- have difficulty with? _____
- not enjoy? _____

How do you think you relate with:
- other staff? _____
- other senior staff? _____
- your employer? _____

Have you any skills, knowledge or abilities not being used fully in your job?

_____

What are they and how can we use them? _____

What training have you had this year? _____

What aspects of this training have you been able to apply to your job?

_____

What training needs do you have which would enable you to do your job better?

_____

How do you see your career progressing? _____

Action agreed with targets and dates _____

Signed _____ Supervisor

Signed _____ Member of Staff

Date _____

Figure 4.30

Staff appraisal form

Lucas Varity plc uses the following as part of its performance appraisals for managers:

1 executives appraise themselves
2 they have an appraisal interview with their immediate line manager
3 they undertake a series of psychometric tests
4 an independent consultant appraises their performance against managers in similar companies.

Exit reviews

When staff leave an employer there is an opportunity to receive an objective evaluation of the business. Exit interviews can be used to try to find out:

- the real reasons why employees are leaving
- the strengths and weaknesses of the organisation
- whether low morale, poor wages or poor conditions are a factor.

Few organisations act on the information they receive as it may be difficult to analyse its validity and reliability.

Key terms

Motivation explains why a person chooses to act in particular ways. If an employer knows what motivates you, then they are able to make you work harder, ensure you enjoy your job and encourage you to change your attitude to work.

Job enrichment is a method of changing the design and experience of work to improve motivation and performance.

I Motivation

There are several theories about what motivates people and the importance of financial incentives.

Scientific management

Frederick Taylor's 'Principles of Scientific Management' recognised that most employees took manual jobs in factories and administrative jobs in offices because they were motivated by the financial rewards. He thought jobs should be designed on the following scientific principles:

- clear division of tasks and responsibilities between management and workers
- scientific selection and training of the workforce
- development of standard procedures and rules for work
- managers should always be in full control
- enthusiasm and cooperation of the workforce, which is achieved using financial incentives.

In Taylor's view workers' primary incentive is money. However, critics argue that this approach means that work is boring and repetitive, and the individual's role in the organisation is small and meaningless. Monotony creates apathy, dissatisfaction and carelessness and individuals develop no skills which might lead to promotion. It may create efficient ways of working but it's not very motivating.

Hierarchy of needs

Maslow, in his Hierarchy of Needs, argued that we have seven inborn needs which are organised in a loose hierarchy or order of importance (see Figure 4.31).

Each of these needs can be met, though different needs are met in different ways. For example:

- Private health insurance
- Good working conditions
  good wages / salary
  cheap mortgages
  subsidised food
  attractive pension
  safe working conditions
  no redundancy policy
- Sports & Social Clubs
  office parties, barbecues
  permission for informal activities
  encouraging open communication

- Regular, positive feedback from
  appraisal
  prestigious job titles
  features in organisation's
  magazine
  promotions
- Challenging work projects
  discretion over work activities
  promotion opportunities
  encouraging creativity.

What about the top two aspects of motivation? These were regarded by Maslow as essential for the satisfaction of the first five needs.

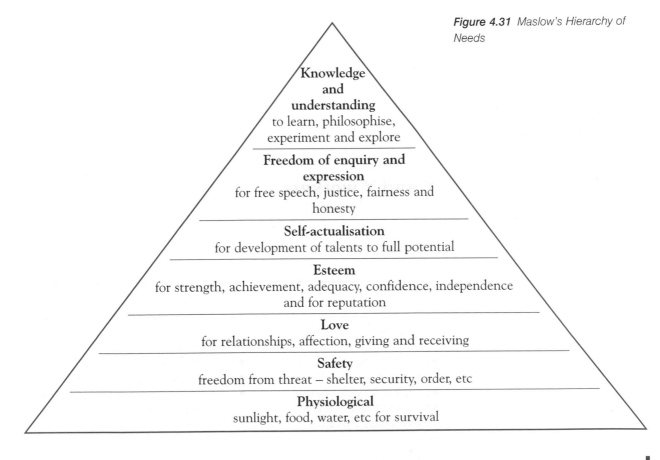

Figure 4.31 *Maslow's Hierarchy of Needs*

Knowledge and understanding
to learn, philosophise, experiment and explore

Freedom of enquiry and expression
for free speech, justice, fairness and honesty

Self-actualisation
for development of talents to full potential

Esteem
for strength, achievement, adequacy, confidence, independence and for reputation

Love
for relationships, affection, giving and receiving

Safety
freedom from threat – shelter, security, order, etc

Physiological
sunlight, food, water, etc for survival

Motivators

As an antidote to Taylor, theories developed around the phrase 'job enrichment', first coined and developed by US psychologist Frederick Hertzberg in the 1950s. It has resulted in some of today's rewards such as flexitime. Hertzberg developed the 'Two Factor Theory of Motivation'. From his research he argued that events which led to job satisfaction were called 'motivators', e.g.:

Achievement	Recognition	Responsibility
Advancement	Growth	The work itself

Events which led to dissatisfaction were called 'hygiene' factors, e.g.:

Salary	Company policy	Supervision
Status	Security	Working conditions

Thus job satisfaction and dissatisfaction arise from differing not opposing factors.

Hertzberg argued that improvement in hygiene factors might alleviate but not cure dissatisfaction. The redesign of jobs to increase motivation and performance should therefore focus on the motivators.

Hertzberg suggested that the following factors would help organisations to achieve job enrichment:

- remove controls
- increase accountability
- create natural working units
- provide direct feedback
- introduce new tasks
- allocate special assignments
- grant additional authority.

The drawback of his theory is that it assumes people must fulfil themselves through work but someone could equally find fulfilment in absenteeism or sabotage!

X and Y workers

Douglas McGregor contrasted two sets of assumptions about the attitude of workers.

Table 4.11 McGregor's Theory X and Theory Y

Theory X	Theory Y
Reluctant worker who has to be offered rewards	Keen worker who loves work
These people: • hate work • are unambitious, lazy and not very dependable • need to be controlled • concentrate on satisfying their needs of nature	These people: • enjoy work • like and seek responsibility • don't like being controlled • concentrate on satisfying social and self-actualising needs

This theory is similar to Herzberg's in that Theory X workers want pay and need the threat of punishment whereas Y workers like work and that is a motivator.

ACTIVITY

Which category would you fall in to (X or Y)?

Many other theories exist about what motivates people – the ones above are most talked about and generally regarded as the most influential. Essentially they recognise that people have certain needs and that an employer must make sure that these needs are satisfied if employees are to feel motivated to do their jobs well. Different organisational cultures encourage different patterns of motivation in their workplaces.

Motivated staff are important to organisations since they:
- do their jobs more efficiently and effectively
- feel more loyalty to their employers
- think of ways of improving what they do
- have higher attendance and punctuality rates.

One role of human resource management is to identify what motivates people and, where possible, provide these things for employees.

Figure 4.32 Which jobs matter the most?

At the most basic level, people go to work in order to earn money and an employer needs to ensure that it pays a suitable amount to its employees. What is suitable will depend upon the nature of the work, the market rate for that type of work and what other motivators may exist. For instance, a large chemicals company pays its relatively unskilled production staff almost twice as much as its more skilled and qualified administrative staff. Reasons for this are that the administrative staff benefit from more interesting and varied jobs, they work in more pleasant conditions and they perceive there to be more status attached to their jobs as office workers.

If you think about how much of your life you could spend at work, you can see that work can have a major effect on your life. Earning a good wage may be satisfying in that it enables you to enjoy your time out of work but it does not help to make the time you spend at work more fulfilling. Because of the amount of time spent at work many people want to regard work as a place where they feel 'at home'. They want to have friends there and they like to feel that they belong to a group (whether that is a work team, a department or a company). They want to feel that working gives them status and that the work they do is valued.

Other people are even more interested in finding work that is challenging and which enables them to use their abilities fully. Sometimes these people put this above earning money. Many actors, for instance, are prepared to go without employment (and earnings) for long periods of time in order to have the opportunity to do something they find really fulfilling. Likewise people often choose to go into less well paid professions such as nursing rather than better paid but less fulfilling ones.

There are many needs that affect why people work and what jobs they do and each person may have a different set of needs. Employers therefore have to be able to offer opportunities that meet these needs in order to motivate staff. Some of these factors will be financial in nature but a good employer will try to provide a balance of financial and non-financial benefits. Besides being more likely to lead to job satisfaction, it can be a lot cheaper. For instance, who hasn't felt good when praised for working well? Praise does not cost the business a penny.

Many of the most powerful motivators have no direct costs associated with them. However, some of them may have an indirect effect on the efficiency of the company's operations. These include:
- job security
- interesting and varied work
- participation in decision-making
- working in teams
- receiving feedback on performance, e.g. through an appraisal scheme
- good relationships with colleagues.

The types of financial factors which can improve job satisfaction include:

- a decent wage package
- different benefits such as pensions, save as you earn schemes, private health care
- commission or performance related pay
- profit sharing
- bonuses.

Other benefits may not involve direct payment of money to employees but do have an obvious financial cost to the employer:

- coffee and tea facilities, canteens, staff lounges and social clubs
- comfortable working conditions
- recognition of good work through promotion or pay rises
- participation in the ownership of the company through employee share schemes
- good holiday entitlements
- sufficient training.

CASE STUDY

Some employers now provide what has been become known as flexible 'cafeteria benefits'. They recognise that different people have different needs and they organise a variety of different benefits from which employees can choose up to an agreed financial value. Someone nearing retirement may choose to have enhanced pension benefits, whereas a young health-conscious employee may instead select reduced membership rates at a local health club.

Texas Instruments' flexible options programme was introduced three years ago and allows staff to spend a portion of their annual salary on holidays, a company pension, a company car, or extra time off to care for children or dependants. While employees must take a minimum of 15 days leave a year they are allowed to 'buy' up to 30 days. The fewer days they opt for the more they can spend on other options or take home in their pay packets.

More than 20 per cent of companies offer flexible benefits and this is growing.

One of the biggest problems with such a scheme is that staff may opt to take less leave because of the relentless pressure of work. Research shows that almost 50 per cent of senior managers and 40 per cent of middle managers do not take their holiday entitlement. Nearly half of those surveyed who did take holidays said their companies phoned them at home. Although 'buying' cash instead of taking a break is tempting, remember 'Nobody ever died wishing they'd spent more time at work'.

This book covers an area of rapidly changing practice besides giving tips, help and advice.

When you've finished studying, what happens if you keep getting rejection letters from employers?

- Keep bouncing back!
- Try temping until something more permanent comes along. It will improve your skills and marketability.
- Structure your day and stick to it.

Remember you've got lots of talent and skills, and you are only just beginning the search for the job that is right for you!

Appendix

Key Legislation

Disability Discrimination Act (1995)

This gives people with disabilities new rights in three main areas:
- employment
- access to goods, facilities and services
- the management, buying or renting or property.

Discrimination occurs when, for a reason related to his or her disability, a person is treated less favourably than other people and this treatment cannot be justified. The Act also set up the National Disability Council to advise the government on discrimination against people with disabilities.

Employers Liability (Compulsory Insurance) Act (1969)

This Act places a duty on employers to take out and maintain approved insurance policies with authorised insurers against liability for bodily injury or disease sustained by employees in the course of their employment.

Employment Protection (Consolidation) Act (1978)

This Act sets out the framework for employees to obtain compensation or reinstatement through an Employment Tribunal if they have been unfairly dismissed. This gives employees the right:
- not to join a trade union on religious grounds
- to join a trade union
- not to be unfairly selected for redundancy
- to be able to return to work following maternity leave
- not to be dismissed for strike action if other employees who also went on strike have not been sacked.

Equal Pay Acts (1970, 1984)

The 1970 Equal Pay Act was introduced to end discrimination between men and women, in basic rates of pay and other terms of their contract of employment (e.g. overtime rates, bonus agreements, holiday entitlements, etc). This was amended in 1984, as a result of European Community legislation, to enable men and women to claim equal wages for work of equal value done for the same employer or an associated employer. Any employee can claim equal pay if the work done is:
- of 'like work' to that of a colleague of opposite sex
- equally rated under a proper job evaluation study
- of equal value in terms of the demands made.

Health and Safety (First Aid) Regulations (1981)

The Regulations require that all businesses must have an appropriate level of first aid treatment available in the workplace. This means that businesses must:

- appoint a person to take charge in an emergency and look after first aid equipment; there must be an 'appointed person' available at all times during working hours
- provide and maintain a First Aid box containing information/guidance on the treatment of injured people
  - how to control bleeding
  - how to give artificial respiration
  - how to deal with unconsciousness
- display notices which state:
  - locations of first aid equipment
  - name of person(s) responsible for First Aid.

Health and Safety at Work Act (1974) (updated by Workplace Health and Safety Welfare Regulations 1992 (EC Directives))

Employers should ensure the provision of adequate toilets and washing facilities, machines that are electrically safe, and protective clothing or equipment; they must ensure that precautions are taken when using chemicals; they must provide and a clean and tidy workplace for their workforce. The self-employed, home workers and people who work alone away from employer's premises are included.

Employers are required to:
- provide systems of work that are, so far as is reasonably practicable, safe and without risk to health.

Employees have responsibility to:
- take reasonable care of themselves and other people affected by their work
- co-operate with their employers in the discharge of their legal obligations.

Human Rights Act (1998)

This came into effect in October 2000 and covers everything a public authority (local government, national government, government agency, etc) does. It provides a basis for the protection of fundamental rights of every citizen. All public authorities have an obligation to ensure that respect for human rights is at the core of their day-to-day work. Questions that public authorities need to ask, include:
- Is a person's ability to carry out a trade or profession affected?
- Is a person's physical or mental well-being affected?
- Is a person's private or family life affected?
- Is any individual or group being discriminated against, on any basis?

If the answer to these types of question is yes, an individual may be able to bring legal action against the public authority.

Offices, Shops and Railway Premises Act (1963)

The Act stipulates minimum standards to ensure a safe and healthy working environment. In conjunction with the Health and Safety at Work Act, it relates to every part of a business's premises.

Businesses should also make provision for a clean, tidy, well lit, well ventilated and well maintained workplace, a clean and tidy workforce, adequate toilet and washing facilities, machines that are electrically safe, protective clothing or equipment, control of noise and vibration, accident and fire prevention, the safe use of chemicals and dangerous substances, and the safe transport and handling of materials.

Race Relations Act (1976)

This Act defines three types of discrimination, all of which are illegal:

- direct discrimination which treats a person on racial grounds less favourably than others are or would be treated in the same circumstances
- indirect discrimination which applies a requirement or condition which, whether intentionally or not, adversely affects a particular racial group considerably more than others
- discrimination by means of victimisation by treating a person less favourably than others because that person has made a complaint or allegation of discrimination.

The Act also established the Commission for Racial Equality which has direct responsibility for monitoring the effect of the Act.

Reporting of Injuries, Diseases and Dangerous Occurrences Regulations (1985)

These Regulations cover occupational disease, serious injury or death in connection with a business. A report must be sent to the local authority if:

- death or serious injury occurs in an accident at work
- anyone is off work for more than three days as a result of an accident at work
- specified occupational disease is certified by a doctor.

Employers are required to record in an accident book any accident or case of disease requiring to be reported (preferably signed by all parties concerned).

Sex Discrimination Acts (1975, 1986)

These Acts declare that it is unlawful to be less favourably treated because of your sex or marital status. Discrimination can be considered under two headings:

- direct discrimination occurs if you are treated less favourably than a person of the opposite sex is (or would be) treated in similar circumstances
- indirect discrimination occurs when you are unable to comply with a requirement, which on the face of it seems to apply equally to both sexes, but which in practice can be met only by a much smaller proportion of one sex.

Trade Union and Labour Relations (Consolidation) Act (1992)

The Act provides protection for employees who were dismissed for being members of trade unions.

Trade Union Reform and Employment Rights Act (1993)

This entitles every employee who works for more than sixteen hours a week to an itemised pay slip at or before the payment of every salary.

Transfer of Undertakings Regulations (1981)

These regulations provide employees with protection when their business is taken over by new employers. Prior to the regulations (usually referred to as TUPE), an employee's existing conditions and terms of employment would not be transferred to a new employer. All employees were considered as having no statutory rights associated with continuity of employment. This was changed with the European Union's Acquired Rights Directive in 1997 which provided:

- that employment contracts are automatically transferred from one employer to another
- protection from dismissal as a result of, or for reasons related to, the transfer
- that employers are obliged to inform and consult with employees' representatives before the transfer.

Unfair Contracts Terms Act (1977)

This prevents anyone from including an unreasonable clause in a contract.

Wages Act (1986)

This Act restricts the employer from taking money from the employee's wages unless the deduction is:

- a legal requirement
- part of the employee's contract and the employee has been notified in writing
- agreed to by the employee in writing.

Index